The Case
of the
Curious Campaign

Robert
Mandelberg

Illustrated by Martin Jarrie

Sterling Publishing Co., Inc.
New York

To my wife Jan-Nika: dresser of windows,
    singer of Romemu, possessor of sweetness,
    and solver of life s mini-mysteries.

A snooty thank you to fancy lady Nancy Sherman for
    one finely manicured pinkie raised elegantly skyward.

Edited by Nancy E. Sherman

Library of Congress Cataloging-in-Publication Data Available

10   9   8   7   6   5   4   3   2

Published by Sterling Publishing Co., Inc.
387 Park Avenue South, New York, NY 10016
' 2003 by Rober t Mandelberg
Distributed in Canada by Sterling Publishing
℅ Canadian Manda Group, 165 Dufferin Street
Toronto, Ontario, Canada M6K 3H6
Distributed in Great Britain and Europe by Chris Lloyd at Orca Book
Services, Stanley House, Fleets Lane, Poole BH15 3AJ, England
Distributed in Australia by Capricorn Link (Australia) Pty. Ltd.
P.O. Box 704, Windsor, NSW 2756, Australia

Sterling ISBN 1-4027-0382-1

Contents

Tuesday

Background

"The Busy Body Detective Agency," read the lettering on the glass door. Inside was a plush reception area with four cozy leather chairs, a matching couch, a good number of very costly-looking accessories, and a sleek mahogany reception desk. Behind the desk sat the agency's part-time receptionist and office manager, Ms. Annie Body. Annie was as sleek as her desk, with long red hair and a magnetic smile. On the wall behind Annie hung a picture of the president of the Busy Body Detective Agency, Mr. Avery Body. Avery was Annie's father.

The tall, distinguished gentleman who entered the Busy Body Detective Agency that sunny Tuesday morning was Mr. Hugh Ever, the popular and good-looking mayor of Wellington, who was running for re-election in a hotly contested race. The mayor had perfect, slightly graying hair held stiffly in place by ample hair spray. He was in a somber mood, and for good reason.

The election was coming down to the wire—it was exactly a week away—and the two candidates were neck and neck in the polls. In fact, the mayor was seriously concerned that he was about to lose. He approached Annie to explain that he needed to speak with Avery right away. Even his rather desperate circumstance, however, could not keep him from flirting with the vivacious receptionist.

"You're looking radiant today, Annie. Maybe after I win the election we can talk about a position for you in my organization."

Annie brushed aside the comment as she smiled and pressed a button on the intercom. "Daddy, Mayor Ever is here to see you."

A moment later, Avery burst into the reception area and gave Mayor Ever a warm greeting and a hearty handshake. Avery was a rotund man in his 50s with a jovial face, a protruding nose, and rosy cheeks. The little hair he had left formed a thin, graying semicircle around the sides of his head. "Well, well, well! If it isn't our esteemed mayor! What brings you...?"

Hugh Ever interrupted Avery mid-sentence, peering at his friend with a look of terror. "Avery, we need to talk."

Avery saw that Hugh was anxious so he quickly escorted him into his richly furnished private corner office. Hugh Ever strode briskly through the threshold and paced around the room. "Avery, I've gotten in way over my head, I'm afraid. I don't know where to turn."

"Now, now, Hugh. Have a seat and let's sort this all out," Avery said in his most reassuring tone. "Hugh, we've known each other for a long time. We've gotten out of some pretty tight spots in the past."

Hugh sat down across the desk from Avery and leaned forward. "I know what you're trying to do, Avery. And I appreciate it. But this time it's different. I think everything is lost. He has me right where he wants me."

Avery was confused. "Who has you? What are you talking about?"

"Quentin. Quentin Milestone, that's who!" Hugh was practically shouting. "Apparently he has information about my past and if I don't withdraw from the race, he'll expose me."

Quentin Milestone was the owner of the Top Cat Barber Shop and the only other candidate running for mayor. He had run against Hugh Ever unsuccessfully in the previous two elections and sworn publicly that he would do anything to win this time around.

Avery opened a silver case on his desk and extracted a pair of cigars. He lit one and offered the other to his friend. Hugh declined. "Why are you so worried?" Avery said, as he puffed on his stogie. "I'm sure that Milestone is just bluffing. You can't let him get to you like this. You're an honest, upright citizen of this community. You have a clean past and nothing to hide, right?"

Hugh was silent.

"Right, Hugh?" Avery repeated. Continued silence. "Hugh???"

"To tell you the truth, Avery, I don't know what information he has. I checked all of my sources and informants, but I came up with nothing. My biggest fear is that something horrible will appear in  the newspaper, and I'll lose the race. I need your help." Hugh Ever was clearly exasperated.

"You can count on me, my friend. My detective agency is at your disposal." Avery had always campaigned enthusiastically for his friend Hugh. He was his most ardent supporter. Avery pressed the intercom button. "Annie, will you call Noah and Sam in here right away?"

Noah and Sam were Avery's sons and worked at the agency as junior detectives. Sam was the first to arrive. He was a well-built young man, 25 years old, with short, wavy brown hair and turquoise eyes. Sam was a bright, inquisitive investigator who had a knack for uncovering secrets and solving mysteries. Hugh

Ever had always liked Sam and had talked to him several times about pursuing a career in politics.

Noah arrived a minute later. He was Sam's senior by two years. In many ways, Noah was Sam's exact opposite. While Sam was handsome, charming, and ethical, Noah was awkward, arrogant, and sarcastic, with a reputation for being sly and cold-hearted. When the Busy Body Detective Agency had a dirty job to be performed, it was Noah who carried it out.

mystery *1

Molly the Snitch:

Avery locked the door and called Annie on the intercom. "Annie, darling, hold all calls, please."

Hugh loosened his tie and began to provide details about his situation with Quentin to the three detectives. Avery, Sam, and Noah pulled out their pads and wrote furiously. Avery asked Hugh how he found out that Quentin had information about him.

Hugh Ever stood and resumed his pacing. "Well, since the election against Quentin was so close four years ago, I decided that I couldn't afford to take any chances this time around. So I struck a deal with one of his employees to feed me information."

"Why, of all the low-down, dirty, underhanded tricks!" cried Noah. "I am very impressed! What a terrific idea!"

Hugh continued: "Molly Peltin, a hair stylist at Quentin's barber shop, told me that while she was working on a customer yesterday afternoon, she heard Quentin whispering on the telephone across the room."

"What was he saying?" Sam inquired.

Hugh sat back down. "She said that Quentin was talking to a newspaper reporter and discussing the election. She heard Quentin say that he had some dirt on me that would blow this whole race wide open."

Avery said, "This isn't good, Hugh. Was Molly able to find out anything else?"

"No." Hugh replied. "Molly said that she had no time. She finished blow drying her customer's hair and got ready to see her next appointment. She wasn't able to learn anything more."

The three detectives paused and looked at each other. Avery asked, "Tell me, Hugh, are you paying Molly by the hour or by the story?"

"I pay her for anything she uncovers. Why is that important?" asked the mayor.

Noah smiled and said, "I think you better get your money back, mayor. You've been swindled."

What did Noah mean by that?

answer

Sam said, "Excuse me, Mayor Ever, but did you say that Molly heard Quentin whispering to a reporter on the telephone?"

"Yes. That's what she said. Whispering," retorted Hugh.

Noah walked up to the mayor and said, "Perhaps you can explain to us how Molly was able to hear Quentin whispering clear across the room while she was blow drying someone's hair."

Mayor Ever was stunned. "But why would she...?"

Before he could complete his sentence, Noah chimed in, "For the money, Mayor Ever. That's why. You said yourself that she only gets paid when she gives you information."

Avery walked over to Hugh and slapped his friend on the back. "False alarm, my good friend. It looks like he has nothing on you after all."

▌ Know What You Did

Hugh's expression remained somber. "It's not that simple. You see, Molly isn't the only reason that I think Quentin has something on me." He reached into his pocket and pulled out an envelope. "Read this."

Avery took the envelope from Hugh's trembling hands. He saw that it was addressed to Mayor Ever with no return address. It was postmarked the day before. He removed a letter, unfolded it and read it aloud:

Hugh Ever, you slimy, sleazy, low-life scuzzball! I know what you did! I am on to you! Your secret is out! If you don't drop out of the race at once, I will blab to the papers! Do you hear me? Blab! I know what you did! I'll tell all! Hold on, I have a phone call. I'm back. You're a scuzzball! I am on to you! I know what you did! Drop out!

Sincerely,

Anonymous

P.S. I know what you did!

"Do you see? He knows what I did!" screamed Hugh in terror.

"What did you do?" cried Sam.

"I don't know! But he knows! Did you see the P.S.? What am I going to do? He's going to blab!" cried Hugh. He pulled at his ears, wrung his hands, and sobbed like a baby.

"The first thing you're going to do is relax," said Avery, as he tried to calm his friend. "The writer of this letter doesn't seem to know anything about you or what you allegedly did. It's filled with vague threats and unsubstantiated accusations. I wouldn't pay any attention to them."

The mayor took a few deep breaths in an attempt to settle down. "I hope you're right Avery. The polls are so close, the slightest incident could push it one way or the other." Avery took the letter and put it in a drawer to keep for future reference. "When I received this letter last week, I thought it was just a hoax.

But after Molly told me about Quentin's conversation with a reporter, I was scared that it might be related."

"Well, like I said," Avery replied, "I'm sure it's nothing, but just to be safe, my boys and I will look into it for you."

"Thank you, Avery. You have no idea how much this means to me," Hugh said as he stood up and shook Avery's hand. He said his goodbyes to the three detectives and left the office.

Avery, Sam, and Noah sat down around Avery's desk. Sam said to his father, "What's the plan?"

"The first thing we're going to do," Avery responded, "is find out why my friend is lying to us."

Sam and Noah looked at each other. "Lying?!" they said in unison.

Why did Avery think Hugh was lying?

answer

"You think he's lying? How can you say such a thing?" Sam asked in confusion. "Mayor Ever wouldn't lie to us."

Avery looked as his son and said, "Sam, I don't want to believe it either, but it's true. Remember when he said that he received the letter last week?"

"Yes, he said he thought it was a hoax at first."

"He did, yes. I'm not questioning that. But I saw the envelope; it was postmarked yesterday, October 25th! How could he have received the letter last week if it had yesterday's date stamped on it by the post office?"

"That devious, two-faced politician!" Noah exclaimed in outrage. "I'm starting to like that man more and more."

Sam was quick to defend Hugh Ever's actions. "I think that if Mayor Ever lied to us, it must be because he is in deep trouble and needs our help."

"I agree with you, Sam," said his father, "and we're going to do whatever we can to help him."

The Pushy Reporter

"Good morning, Chollie," said the rawboned, skinny man in his late 20s as he entered the Busy Body Detective Agency. He wore a derby and carried a notepad in his shirt pocket. "Is your boss here? I need to talk to him right away, Chollie."

"Mr. Body is in a meeting and can't be disturbed," said Annie with a smile. "And my name's not Chollie. It's Annie."

The man wasn't swayed by Annie's cheery disposition. "Yeah, listen Chollie, I got urgent business to discuss with your boss. So what do you say you just press your little intercom button and tell him he has a visitor."

"Sir, you can wait if you like, but I can't disturb him now," was Annie's reply.

"I hate waiting," said the man. "It makes my migraine act up." The man reached into his pocket and pulled out a small red pill. "Tell me, Chollie, is this pill green?"

Annie leaned over to inspect it. "No, it's red."

"Whew, that was close, Chollie," said the man. "I almost mixed up my headache pill with my sleeping pill. I would have been out like a light! You see, I'm color blind, and I can't pick out certain colors. I guess I took the wrong one with me today."

"I'm sorry to hear that," Annie sympathized.

"Yeah, listen, Chollie. See, I'm a reporter, and if you don't let me in to talk to your boss pronto, I'm gonna give this agency a write-up that will put you out of business in a week. You don't want that on your conscience, do ya?"

Annie thought that she better let her father decide whether or not to see him. Avery was still talking with his sons and planning a strategy for the mayor when the intercom buzzed. "Daddy." Annie's voice filled the room. "A very pushy reporter is in the reception area. I told him you were in a meeting, but he insists on talking to you."

A moment later the door swung open and the reporter burst into the room. "What are you doing here?" Sam said in a disgusted tone of voice. "How dare you show your face in this office!"

Sam was directing his remarks to Bob Crook, the reporter from *The Daily Sentinel*. Three weeks earlier, Sam and Bob had had a run-in during an investigation of a kidnapping case involving Nicole Stewart, the daughter of Governor Keith Stewart. Bob Crook had pretended to befriend Sam, and tricked him into revealing specific details about the case. Just as Sam was closing in on the kidnapper, Bob Crook printed the entire story on the front page of his newspaper. The kidnapper got away and Nicole had not been seen since. Until that time, the governor had been an active campaigner for Quentin Milestone. After the kidnapping, he stopped supporting Quentin completely.

"I'm here on business, Chollie," replied the reporter.

Sam rose from his chair and stood face-to-face with Bob. Avery inserted his enormous self between the two young men to put some distance between them. He turned to the reporter. "Mr. Crook, what business do you have with us today?"

Bob Crook gestured toward a chair, but no one offered him a seat. He decided to speak his mind while standing. "I'll be brief, Chollies. I've been following the mayor all morning and I noticed him coming out of your office. I'd like to know if he hired your agency for anything."

His words burned in Sam's ears. "You creep! What business do you have following around Mayor Ever? You're lucky I don't...."

Avery put his hand up to quiet his rambunctious son.

Bob Crook continued: "Relax, Chollie. I'm just doing my job. The election is exactly one week away and I'm supposed to find out what I can about the candidates. I already found out quite a bit about the mayor."

"Such as?" Noah inquired.

"Well, for starters," Bob Crook said, "Mayor Ever withdrew $100,000 from his bank account and made a payoff to Carrie Renz, the election official."

The three detectives sat there dumbfounded. "This is quite disturbing. How do you know this?" Avery demanded.

Bob Crook, sensing their interest, took the liberty to sit down, even though he was not invited to do so. He said, "My cousin, Little Frankie, came into town two days ago for a few hours to ask me about getting him a job at my newspaper. As it turns out, he's gonna make one sharp reporter some day. He told me that on his way to see me, he stopped by the bank to withdraw some money to take me to lunch. Little Frankie said that he was in line behind Mayor Ever and heard him ask the teller for $100,000 in large bills.

"Then yesterday morning, I followed the mayor to an abandoned warehouse on the edge of town. He met Carrie Renz there and handed her a package. Although I'm sure I saw the mayor and Ms. Renz, I was parked too far away to hear what they were saying. And knowing that he had just withdrawn all that money from his account, I assumed that's what he was giving the election official." He paused and smugly clasped his hands behind his head. "So, detectives, how's that for some fancy investigative work?"

The detectives could not help but burst into laughter. Finally Sam caught his breath and blurted, "Better not quit your day job."

What was wrong with Bob Crook's story?

"What's that supposed to mean?" asked Bob Crook.

"Don't you even know what day it is?" asked Noah. "Let me help you. You said yourself that the election is exactly one week away from today, and since elections are always held on Tuesdays, today must be Tuesday."

"Yeah, so?" said Bob Crook.

Sam joined in. "You said that Little Frankie was in town two days ago. Tell me, does Little Frankie often go to the bank on Sundays when they're closed? I don't know about you, but I prefer to wait until the bank is open to make my withdrawals."

The expression on the young reporter's face turned to embarrassment. "I can't believe I let Little Frankie pull one over on me. Okay, I admit that I may have been wrong about the money, but I know what I saw. Mayor Ever handed the election official a package."

"That is certainly worth investigating," Avery proclaimed. "Well, we appreciate your stopping by, Mr. Crook. I think you know the way out."

Bob Crook stood up and made his way out of Avery's office. But not before he dropped his notepad on the floor. When he bent down to pick it up, his hand slipped under his chair momentarily. Avery noticed this, but didn't think anything of it at the time.

As soon as the reporter left, the three Bodys made their plan. They reviewed all of the clues and Avery reread Hugh's letter out loud. They then decided that they would start the investigation the next day. Sam and Noah would find out what they could from the election official, while Avery would pay a visit to Quentin Milestone to see if he knew anything about Mayor Ever. The three detectives agreed to meet at Sophie's Diner at 12:00 to discuss what they learned.

Wednesday

The Election Official & Mr. Pock

Next morning, Sam and Noah drove to Borough Hall to pay a visit to Carrie Renz, the election official. They were intent on discovering whether or not Ms. Renz had had a secret rendezvous at an abandoned warehouse with the mayor, as alleged by the reporter.

The two men entered the election official's office to see a short, stocky clerk in his mid-thirties standing behind a tall counter. The nameplate on the counter indicated he was Mr. Pock. One look at Mr. Pock told you that he hated his job. His eyes drooped, he spoke with a slow drawl, and he yawned every 30 seconds or so. Talking to this man for more than three minutes was enough to make one's brain explode from sheer, excruciating boredom.

An elderly gentleman was asking this clerk for assistance and was rapidly approaching the three-minute brain explosion limit. Mr. Pock said, "I am very sorry, Mr. Spinn. This is not the tax office (yawn). You have to go down to the end of the hall and make a right." He spoke just 27 words, but it took a full minute and a half to say them. Mr. Spinn slowly turned around and left.

Noah and Sam approached the clerk with polite smiles. Noah took the lead saying, "Good morning, my name is Noah Body. This is my brother, Sam. We'd like to speak with Ms. Renz, please."

16

Mr. Pock summoned all the energy he could muster and pressed the intercom button. "Ms. Renz, Noah Body is here to see you."

"Nobody is here to see me?" was the response over the intercom. "So, why are you bothering me?"

"Because he wants to see you (yawn)," replied Mr. Pock.

Ms. Renz was already sounding irritated. "Who?"

"Noah Body," answered Mr. Pock in a painfully slow voice.

Ms. Renz shouted, "If nobody wants to see me, why are you bothering me, Mr. Pock?"

Sam interrupted. "This is getting us nowhere. I am Sam Body, Noah's brother. Please tell Ms. Renz that I am here to see her."

Mr. Pock complied. He pressed the talk button and said, "Sam Body wants to see you."

"Somebody wants to see me? Pock, you are getting on my nerves!" Ms. Renz barked. "Who is it?"

"Sam Body," said Mr. Pock.

"Never mind, you idiot! I'm coming out!" In a matter of seconds, Carrie Renz came briskly through the office door.

"Good morning, Ms. Renz," said Sam with a bright smile. "Thank you for taking the time to speak with us."

Carrie Renz's hair was pulled back in a bow so tight, it caused her eyes to stretch wide. She was an otherwise attractive woman in her early forties but very short tempered. Ms. Renz had developed the reputation of a mean-spirited divorcee who refused to put up with any nonsense.

"What is it, gentlemen? I don't have a lot of time to waste," snapped Ms. Renz.

Noah knew how to deal with people like her. "Well then, let me get right to the point. We have knowledge that you and Mayor Ever had a clandestine meeting on Monday. We were hoping that you could tell us a little about that."

"I don't have a clue what you're talking about. Why on earth would I want to meet with Mayor Ever?" responded Ms. Renz.

"Oh, come now, Ms. Renz," Noah said with a sarcastic smile. "There's no point in hiding it. We have an eyewitness who saw you speaking with Hugh Ever. We also understand that he handed you a package."

"Now you're talking rubbish," grunted Ms. Renz. "I would never do such a thing. I am the election official and Mayor Ever is running for reelection. I'd have to be out of my mind to meet with a candidate at some warehouse. And I don't like the implication that I took a bribe."

Just then Mr. Pock interrupted the conversation. He inhaled deeply so as to say what he needed to in a single breath. He couldn't bear the thought of having to summon the energy required to take a second one. He yawned and said, "Ms. Renz, there's a call for you. It's an emergency. It seems that Mr. Spinn's head has exploded in the hallway."

"Not another one." The election official turned to the detectives and said, "I'm sorry to cut this short, boys, but I have to take this call. Too bad I couldn't be any help."

Sam said, "That's just fine, Ms. Renz. You've helped us more than you know." Satisfied, Noah and Sam turned to leave.

What was Sam implying?

answer

The two young detectives left the office and had a chat in the hallway. Sam said, "I don't recall your telling Ms. Renz that the meeting was at a warehouse. Did you mention that?"

"No," Noah replied. "She offered that tidbit herself."

Sam grinned. "I thought so! Now at least we know that the reporter was telling the truth. Mayor Ever and the election official did have a secret meeting."

Noah and Sam strode triumphantly out of Borough Hall. As soon as they stepped outside, they noticed a beautiful young woman attempting to change her tire. The two boys walked over to offer their assistance.

Quentin Milestone

While Sam and Noah were busy at Borough Hall that Wednesday morning, Avery set out to complete his assignment to discover what dirt Quentin Milestone had on Mayor Hugh Ever. It was approximately 10:15 A.M. when he parked his oversized white Cadillac in the lot in front of the Top Cat Barber Shop and removed his oversized self from the vehicle. Avery said hello and tipped his hat to a young mother walking her twin boys in a stroller. Whistling "Fugue for Tinhorns," a catchy tune from *Guys and Dolls,* he gaily strode into the shop.

Avery was immediately greeted by Molly Peltin. "Good morning, Mr. Body. I didn't see you in the appointment book. Are you here for a haircut?"

"Yes, Molly, I decided to stop by on a whim. I know there's not much left to work with," said Avery with a smile, "but I was thinking of trimming it up a little. Is Quentin around?"

"He's in his office, Mr. Body. Let me tell him you're here." Molly scooted to the back while Avery looked around the shop. A moment later, Quentin Milestone emerged from the back room, his face arranged in a transparent smile. He was an unusual-looking gentleman, with a head that was disproportionately large for his body. He had a long forehead, short brown hair, and wore a barber's apron. Quentin Milestone was 52 years old. In a loud, jovial tone, Quentin greeted Avery. "Well, helllllooooooo, my good friend, Avery!"

Good friend, now that was a laugh! Avery and Quentin Milestone had been neighbors growing up. They had had a lot in common, including the fact that they were each an only child. In high school, they were constantly in competition against one another, vying for the best grades, the best friends, even the best dates. Quentin always seemed to come out on top. Soon after they graduated, their long-time rivalry turned bitter as they ended up both dating the same woman, Roberta Rose. After what seemed like an eternity, Roberta finally made up her mind and decided to marry Avery. Quentin was never able to shake the awful humiliation, which is probably why he remained a bachelor his whole life. The two men had learned to be civil to one another, but the old wounds never quite healed. Even after Roberta passed away several years later, relations between them remained cold.

Quentin Milestone squeezed just a little too tight as the two former rivals shook hands. Quentin said, "Don't tell me you're here for a haircut—I thought those days were long gone for you!"

Avery chuckled and retorted, "Actually, I was thinking of getting a perm." Avery was good natured and had a great sense of humor. He enjoyed a good joke, even at his own expense.

The two men shared a forced laugh as Quentin escorted Avery to the last barber's chair. Avery got to work right away. "So, according to the polls, the race for mayor is coming down to the wire."

"Yes, it's very exciting, isn't it?" answered Quentin, as he eyed Avery suspiciously. "Your good friend, Hugh Ever, beat me in the last two elections, but I have a feeling this time it will turn out differently."

"You seem quite confident," observed Avery. "Is there something you know that I don't?"

Just then their conversation was interrupted by the sound of an old, beaten-up car with a bad muffler. The noise emanating from the automobile was so loud, it almost seemed to come from inside the barber shop. A young man exited from the driver's side and walked into the shop without turning off his engine.

Avery recognized him the moment he strode into the shop. It was none other than Bob Crook, the reporter from *The Daily Sentinel*. He was carrying a large envelope under his arm. Crook marched past Molly Peltin with an arrogant "Howya doin', Chollie," and entered the salon area. A harsh, penetrating stench seemed to follow him closely as Bob Crook approached.

"Hello again, Chollie. Quite a strange coincidence to see you here this morning," said the reporter to Avery.

"I was thinking the same thing. Good morning, Mr. Crook," Avery responded.

"Well, Chollie," Bob Crook addressed Quentin with a smirk. "I have something I think you will find very interesting." He handed Quentin the envelope he was carrying. "It's in this gray envelope."

"That envelope is blue," corrected Quentin.

"Whatever, Chollie, gray, blue, what's the difference? Just look inside," snapped Bob Crook.

"What is it?" Quentin inquired. "It stinks to high heaven!"

The reporter said, "It sure does. I found it in your garbage out by the curb."

"My, my," Avery exclaimed in disbelief. "Don't ever let anyone accuse you of having too much integrity, Mr. Crook."

"Thank you for saying so, Chollie," Bob Crook replied, taking Avery's barb as a compliment.

Quentin Milestone was busy opening the envelope and removing its contents. His face lost all color as he removed an 8x10 photograph that had been torn to pieces and then somehow meticulously taped back together. It was a picture of Quentin Milestone holding hands with a young woman who appeared to be approximately 22 years old.

"I found this picture ripped into a million pieces. It took me all night putting it back together. What's the matter, Chollie? Cat got your tongue?" quipped Bob Crook.

Quentin was indeed speechless. "Well, no, I...I am just...I'm just...."

"You're just, you're just, you're just what?" taunted the reporter. "This ain't gonna look so good plastered all over the front page of *The Daily Sentinel* just before the big election, now is it?"

Quentin thought for a moment, regained his composure and said, "Actually, I think it would be great for my campaign. Can you run it tomorrow?"

Bob Crook was puzzled. "Are you out of your brain, Chollie? Running around with a girl less than half your age! Do you know what this scandal will do to your precious campaign? It'll ruin ya! You're gonna be outta the race!"

Quentin laughed. "I hardly think that a picture of me holding hands with my niece is very scandalous."

Again, the reporter was completely deflated. "Huh? Your niece?"

"Yes, of course! And I've been looking all over for that photograph. It must have been destroyed by accident. Thank you."

The young reporter was completely dejected. "Your niece? Oh no. I feel another migraine coming on." Bob Crook reached into his pocket for a headache pill, mumbled his goodbyes, and slunk out of the barber shop. The noise from his jalopy faded as he drove away.

"Imagine that," Quentin chuckled. "He thought he had something on me."

Avery got up from the chair and removed his smock. "Well, Quentin. You may have fooled the reporter, but I didn't buy it for a second. How much do I owe you for the haircut?"

Why didn't Avery believe Quentin's story?

Avery left the barber shop and climbed into his Cadillac to drive to the diner where he was scheduled to meet Noah and Sam. He chuckled as he mentally replayed the conversation with Quentin Milestone. Niece, indeed, he thought. The man has no brothers or sisters and was never married. So how in the world could he possibly have a niece? Avery knew that Quentin was lying about the young woman and looked forward with great excitement to sharing this information with Noah and Sam.

mystery *6

Sophie's Diner

Wellington was a quirky little town with a number of unusual features. One of the oddest aspects of living in this suburb was its situation directly on the boundary of two time zones. The eastern half of the town was in the eastern standard time zone (EST), and the western half of Wellington was in the central standard time zone (CST). Sophie's Diner was positioned directly in the center of town, and stood as the dividing point between the two time zones.

Sophie Turkus, owner of Sophie's Diner, used this peculiarity to her advantage. Although her diner was open from 6 A.M. to 10 P.M., she would open and close according to whichever time zone suited her that day. If she was feeling a bit tired, she would close the diner according to EST, since that was an hour sooner. Many times, surprised customers were whisked out of the diner mid-meal, not fully understanding the time zone switch.

Avery pulled into Sophie's parking lot at exactly 12:00 noon (CST, by the way). This was the time he had arranged to meet his sons to discuss their assignments. Avery strolled into the diner and said hello to Sophie with a pleasant smile.

"How much today, Avery?" asked Sophie, looking at Avery indifferently. The time zone shift was not the only idiosyncracy that distinguished the way Sophie ran her diner. She insisted on finding out ahead of time how much the customer was going to tip, so that she would know what kind of service to provide.

"The usual," replied Avery.

Sophie's look of indifference turned to disappointment as she led Avery to the back of the diner and sat him in the worst booth, facing the parking lot. Although Avery was well liked, he was known around town as a cheapskate.

Avery ordered a cup of coffee and waited patiently for his sons to arrive. After fifteen minutes, he decided to order a second cup. They should have been here by now, thought Avery.

Three cups of coffee later, Avery looked at his watch and noticed that his sons were 45 minutes late. Then he heard tires screeching and looked up to see Noah's Corvette speeding around a corner and into the parking lot. Avery witnessed Noah getting out of the driver's side and pulling a piece of paper out from his pocket. While he was looking at it, Sam walked around to Noah's side of the car and snatched the paper out of his brother's hand. Noah grabbed it back and the two boys proceeded to have an argument in front of the diner. After a few seconds, Avery tapped on the window of the diner to get their attention. Noah quickly put the slip of paper into his pocket as the two boys headed inside.

Noah and Sam sat across from Avery at his booth. "Sorry we're late," said Noah, looking guilty.

"What kept you boys so long?" Avery inquired. "Our meeting was at 12:00 central time."

Noah put on a confused face. "Central time? I could have sworn you said eastern time! Anyway, we came straight here as soon as we finished interviewing the election official."

"I see," said Avery. He noticed that Sam's hands were filthy, covered with some kind of grease. Sam picked up a menu and left a greasy stain on it. "And what was that piece of paper you two were arguing over?"

"Paper? What piece of paper? What are you talking about?" replied Noah, trying to brush the comment aside with a casual laugh. Sam gazed intently at the menu, unable to look his father in the eye.

"Quit stalling," ordered Avery.

Noah relented. "It was nothing. Just a...just a receipt for some groceries."

Avery shook his head and looked at Noah disapprovingly. "I'm disappointed, Noah. I would have thought you could come up with a better story than that. Sam, suppose you tell me what the two of you are hiding from me."

How did Avery know they were hiding something?

"What do you mean hiding? You think I'm lying?" asked Noah indignantly.

"Of course you're lying," snapped Avery. "First of all, if you thought that our meeting was an hour later, you wouldn't have apologized for being late, since you would have been fifteen minutes early."

"I...I merely meant...."

"Secondly," continued Avery, undaunted, "if you had really thought we were supposed to meet at 12:00 eastern time, then you would have been here an hour earlier, not an hour later. And thirdly, when is the last time either one of you ever bought groceries?"

mystery *7

The Distressed Damsel

The boys sat in silence for a moment. Sam finally admitted, "You're right. It is a lie. We knew when we were supposed to meet, but we got distracted."

"I thought so," sighed Avery. "We'll talk about that later, but first tell me what happened at Borough Hall."

Avery's sons instantly became excited as they told their father all about how they tricked the election official, Carrie Renz, into confirming that she met with Mayor Hugh Ever at a warehouse. Avery then told the boys about his meeting with Quentin, the picture found in his trash, and how he was covering up a secret affair with a woman less than half his age.

At this point, the detectives ordered lunch and discussed their next move. Of course, the service was extremely slow, as the three Bodys were sitting in the "lousy tip" section of the diner. While they waited for their order to arrive, they talked about strategy.

Avery said, "We're going to need to investigate this further. I suggest you boys pay another visit to Ms. Renz, only this time, be a little more persuasive." He said this looking at his older son. It had always been Noah's job to be pushy when it was necessary. The detectives agreed to the plan.

Sam rested his hand on the table and left a greasy handprint. He reached for a napkin and got grease all over the napkin holder. He took off his jacket and smeared grease all over that. Whatever he touched, he immediately fouled with his greasy hands. Avery suggested that he wash up before he ruined anything else.

When he returned from the men's room all nice and clean, Avery turned to other matters. "Now that we're caught up on our assignments, suppose you tell me what got you two so distracted before," said Avery curiously.

Sam answered, "Well, as we were leaving the election official's office, we noticed a woman in distress. She was in the parking lot trying to change a tire. The woman said that she had just flown into town and didn't know anyone. She rented a car at the airport, and as she was driving, she heard a 'pop' in one of her tires. So she pulled into the parking lot and tried to change her tire. Noah and I offered to help."

"If you both offered to help, then why were your hands filthy and Noah's so clean?" snorted Avery.

"Well, we both offered to help, but I was the only one actually helping," said Sam. "Noah was trying to get her phone number."

"Was he successful?" asked Avery.

"Yes. When I finished changing her tire, I looked up and saw her pull a piece of paper from her pocket and write something on it. I did all the work, and he got her phone number," said Sam dejectedly. "And what's worse," added Sam, "is that I noticed her tire wasn't even flat. It was all for nothing."

"Fine," said Noah. "You want her number so badly? Here it is." Noah took a piece of paper from his pocket and tossed it on the table. Avery picked it up and looked at it. It was a stark white piece of paper with nothing on it except a telephone number.

Sam took the paper from his father and put it in his pocket. "Fair is fair," said Sam. "After all, I did the work, I deserve her phone number."

Avery chuckled. "Well, Sam, you may deserve the number, but I wouldn't expect her to pick up the telephone when you call."

Why did Avery think that?

answer

"Why is that?" asked Sam. "You mean you think she gave Noah a fake telephone number? I knew it!"

"I wouldn't know about that," said Avery. "But I do know that if this is the same piece of paper you two were grabbing at in the parking lot outside, it would have your greasy fingerprints all over it. All this paper has on it is a telephone number."

The Set-up

Sam looked at Noah accusingly. "So, brother, you pulled the old switcheroo on me. Hand over the real paper."

Noah reached into his pocket and produced another wad of paper, which he placed upon the table. "I hate having a detective for a father," he said.

"But for the record, I was doing fine on my own getting her number without your changing her tire. She was so impressed when I told her how we tricked the election official."

"What?" cried Avery. "Why on earth would you tell her that?"

"Well, she seemed so interested in the election and that I knew so much about it. I told her we were working for the mayor and that he was going to win on Tuesday."

As Avery's face turned red, Noah sensed his dad's displeasure.

"But I think I convinced her that Mayor Ever is the better candidate. And it's a good thing because I saw a 'Vote for Quentin Milestone' bumper sticker on her car as she drove away."

In a restrained voice, Avery said, "That'll be your downfall, young man. The information we uncover is top secret. How many times do I have to tell you that?"

Avery picked up and examined the paper. It appeared to be a page bearing greasy fingerprints, torn from a small notebook. In the center was a telephone number in blue ink and, just below, in a different hand, 'Felicia' was written in pencil. Avery said, "Why is her number written in ink and her name in pencil?"

"She told me her name but I forgot it," said Noah. "She wrote her number with a pen but not her name. Lucky for me I saw her car's license plate read 'Felicia.' I wrote it down with my pencil so I wouldn't forget again."

Avery grumbled, "Well, she certainly put one over on you boys. Let's hope this little episode doesn't cost our friend the election."

Why did Avery suspect Felicia?

"What?" remarked Noah. "Why should the mayor care if she gave us a fake phone number?"

"That wasn't the only fake thing about her," said Avery.

"You mean...?" said Noah.

Avery and Sam looked at Noah in silence for several seconds before Sam said to his brother, "You mean...what?"

Noah said, "I don't know. I was hoping it would look as if I knew what he was talking about."

Avery's expression turned somber. "This Felicia woman was obviously setting you boys up to get information."

"What?!" said the brothers simultaneously.

"Do rental cars usually have election bumper stickers?" Avery asked. "And if that didn't get you rocket scientists suspicious, her vanity license plate certainly should have. Noah, I'm extremely disappointed in you."

Noah blurted, "I messed up," as he pulled out his cell phone to dial the number on the paper. On the third ring, a man answered, "Karsh Real Estate. How can I help you?"

"A fake number, of course," he sighed. "I'm such an idiot." The silence of the others signified their agreement.

"There's something else," he said. "Something peculiar happened before she left."

"What was that?" asked Avery.

"As we were saying goodbye, a mailman approached us and said to Felicia, 'Excuse me, but aren't you friends?' She looked awkward but nodded yes. Then he said, 'I thought so,' and handed Felicia a package. She signed for it and the mailman walked away."

"Hmm, I don't know what to make of that," said Avery. "Let's just have lunch now and think about it later."

A short 45 minutes later, their food arrived. The detectives ate it in silence.

Thursday

The Secretary

Thursday afternoon, a frightened-looking Mayor Hugh Ever walked into the Busy Body Detective Agency, accompanied by his secretary, Lori-Beth Sugarman. Lori-Beth was a young, shapely, gum-chewing blonde who had been working for the mayor for the past six months. Annie had always referred to her as an "airhead." But what she lacked in smarts, she surely compensated for with her looks. Curly flaxen hair, big blue eyes, and a model's figure— these were undoubtedly the qualifications that enticed Hugh into hiring her.

Especially in contrast to the picture of youth and health beside him, the mayor was not looking well. His face was pale and he was visibly shaking.

"Good morning, Mayor Ever, Lori-Beth," smiled Annie as the two of them entered the reception area.

Lori-Beth ignored the greeting. "Yeah (chew, chew), listen Anna...."

"Annie," interrupted Annie.

"Yeah, whatever," continued Lori-Beth, still chewing up a storm. "Anna, the mayor needs to speak to Avery. Run along and get him for us, will ya?"

Annie rolled her eyes and pressed the button on the intercom. "Daddy, Mayor Ever and his, er, secretary are here to see you." Annie turned to Lori-Beth, "You're lucky you caught him. He's leaving early today."

A few seconds later, Avery entered the reception area. "Good morning, Hugh. Good morning, Lori-Beth." He saw that Hugh was white as a ghost. "My word, Hugh! You look awful. What happened?"

Hugh Ever was in shock. All he could do was point to Avery's office while Lori-Beth stood there chewing with great vigor on a small wad of spearmint gum. Avery latched onto Hugh's arm and guided him into his office, leaving Lori-Beth and her gum with Annie. The two gentlemen sat down, and Avery asked his friend what had happened.

"My secretary handed me this letter this morning after the mail arrived. She said it was terrible news, and she wasn't kidding. I was so shaken, I had to have her drive me here today." He presented the letter to Avery, who removed it from the envelope and began reading:

> *Hugh Ever, you no-good, snot-faced slimeball! I told you once to drop out of the race, but did you listen? No!! Don't you understand? I KNOW WHAT YOU DID!!! This is your last chance! I'm watching you, slimeball. When you make a right, I'll be there. When you make a left, I'll be there. And when you fake right and go left, I'll be there, but maybe a step or two late. Drop out now or I'll blab! Hold on, I have an itch. I'm back. Drop out now! No more warnings!!!*
>
> *Sincerely,*
> *Anonymous*
> *P.S. Have a nice day!*

When Avery finished reading the letter, he put it down and looked at the mayor. He said, "Hugh. I'm your friend. Whatever you've gotten yourself into, I can help. But you have to be honest with me. This letter is the same nonsense as the first one you showed me on Tuesday. I know that the first letter was a hoax. It was postmarked the day before you showed it to me, yet you said that you'd had it for a week. So I know that these letters are fakes."

"No, no, Avery, you don't understand," said Hugh.

"What don't I understand? You're not being truthful, Hugh," responded Avery. "How could you have had the letter for a week when it was postmarked the day before?"

"You're right, Avery. I shouldn't have lied to you. I wrote that first letter myself."

"Who, you, Hugh? You? You wrote it? But why?"

"Avery, my good friend, this is so hard to explain. Three months ago, I began dating a very special woman. Our relationship progressed rather quickly, but I had to keep it a secret."

"Why?" inquired Avery, perplexed.

"Avery, please don't judge me. The woman I'm dating is Carrie Renz, the election official. You see, since I'm running for mayor, people might get the wrong idea if they saw me and Carrie together so close to an election."

Avery said, "Ah, yes. That would look a bit suspicious."

Hugh continued, feeling a little more relaxed. "So we would always meet at obscure places where no one would see us. On Monday, it was her birthday, and I met her at an abandoned warehouse outside of town. I had a strange feeling that someone was following me. I was worried that it might have been Quentin Milestone or one of his spies."

"It's all starting to make sense," said Avery. "But why write the fake letter?"

Hugh Ever averted his eyes from Avery and said, "Avery, I needed to know if Quentin Milestone knew about my affair with Carrie. I didn't feel comfortable telling you that I was dating her, so I wrote the letter to get you to investigate the situation. I am ashamed, and I am sorry, my dear friend."

Hugh looked distraught and apologetic. "There, there," said Avery. "I understand. The truth is that you were being followed."

Hugh sprang to his feet. "I knew it! That sneaky, unethical Milestone!"

"No, it wasn't Quentin, Hugh. It was the reporter from *The Daily Sentinel,* Bob Crook. He saw you handing her a package."

"Yes, it was her birthday present!" said Hugh.

Avery smiled and said, "Now it all makes sense. But there's one thing I still don't understand. Why on earth did you write the second letter?"

Mayor Ever leaned in very closely. The color once again faded from his face and his voice quivered as he said, "That's just it. I didn't write the second letter!" The two men stared at each other in silence for several moments.

Avery broke the silence at last, saying, "How can this be?"

Hugh Ever replied, "When I unsealed the envelope and read the letter, I almost fainted. It's so similar to the letter I wrote that whoever wrote it must have known about the first letter. And the only people I told were you, Noah, and Sam."

"I admit that I'm just as perplexed as you," said Avery, crinkling his forehead and rubbing his hairless chin. "I don't know who wrote this second letter, but I do know whom we can ask."

To whom was Avery referring?

Hugh was starting to panic. "Who? Whom can we ask about the letter, Avery?"

Avery replied, "Hugh, how could your secretary have known that the letter was bad news if she handed it to you when it was still sealed?"

The two men paused for a moment and then darted for the door. They tried to pass through the doorway together, but with Avery's girth, this was impossible. Hugh and Avery were stuck there, struggling to break free. Tall Hugh Ever wedged in the doorway next to pudgy Avery Body resembled a giant number 10. Finally they burst into the reception area to find Annie by herself, working at the computer.

"Where did she go?" inquired Hugh.

Annie turned from the computer screen. "Who, Lori-Beth? She got a call on her cell phone and left in a hurry."

Avery asked, "Did she say where she was going?"

"Are you kidding?" snorted Annie. "She didn't even bother to say goodbye."

"This is important, Annie," said Avery. "Tell me everything that went on while we were in my office."

"Well," Annie said, "I tried to make conversation, but she didn't seem very interested. Then her cell phone rang. I heard her say something like 'it should be all clear by 4:00.' Then she hung up and stormed out of the office."

Hugh picked up his hat and made quickly for the door. "I'll go to my office to wait. Maybe she'll go back later."

Avery tried to call Noah on his cell phone to tell him not to go back to the election office. Now that he knew why Hugh Ever and Carrie Renz met at the warehouse, he didn't want his sons interrogating her needlessly. Unfortunately, there was no answer on Noah's cell phone. Avery grabbed his jacket and hat and left the office. A minute later, he was getting into his car and driving down to Borough Hall.

The Return of Mr. Pock

Noah and Sam strode into the election office that Friday afternoon determined to give the third degree to Ms. Renz about her association with Hugh Ever. Upon entering, they found Mr. Pock behind the counter. Pock was speaking to a tall gentleman wearing a derby and carrying a satchel. When Noah and Sam heard the man's voice, they knew his identity immediately. It was Bob Crook, the reporter from the *The Daily Sentinel*. Noah started to approach, but Sam put out his hand to stop him. They decided to stay back instead and just listen to the conversation between Mr. Pock and Bob Crook.

The reporter was apparently trying to persuade Mr. Pock into doing something. They heard him say to Pock, "Tell ya what, I'll give you some valuable items from my own private collection if you'll just tell me everything you know about the candidates."

"I've told you a hundred times, Mr. Crook," said Pock in his agonizingly slow monotone. "Everything that goes on in this office is strictly confidential."

"At least look at what I have to offer," implored Crook. He proceeded to place his bag on the counter and remove its contents. "It's all in my red duffle bag here."

"That bag is blue," corrected Mr. Pock.

"Yeah, whatever, Chollie. Blue, red, magenta, makes no difference, I'm color blind. Look here," Crook continued, "I have in my possession an authentic birth certificate of one of the greatest writers of all time: Mark Twain. Look, it even has his middle name, Steve, which I'm willing to bet most people don't know. I got it when I was writing a feature on American writers. It's worth a fortune."

Pock seemed impressed. "Tempting, but I can't..."

"Wait, you haven't seen the rest," interrupted Crook. He reached into his bag and pulled out an old coin. "This will make your eyes water, Chollie. It's an authentic coin from ancient Rome.

See? You can make out the date on the bottom, 45 B.C., just below the likeness of Julius Caesar."

"Mr. Crook, I already told you..."

"Hold on," interrupted Crook again. He dug into his sack once more and produced a rolled-up piece of parchment paper. "You better sit down for this one, Chollie. I have an original, authentic Declaration of Independence. This was signed by our forefathers on July 4, 1776, and is one of only fourteen in existence. You can clearly read each signature below the typewritten declaration. You'll be the envy of Wellington!"

Pock stood agape, staring at the document. He tried to grasp the parchment but Crook pulled it out of his reach. "Watch it, Chollie, no fingerprints...the oil from your fingers will ruin it." Apparently Bob Crook's fingers did not contain any oil.

"So whattaya say, Chollie? You give me the dirt and these priceless possessions are yours. Do we have a deal?" asked Bob Crook with a disturbing smile.

Pock tapped his cheek as he stood there deep in thought. "I suppose there are some things that aren't completely confidential," he said after long contemplation.

Then Mr. Pock reached out and shook Bob Crook's outstretched hand. The reporter smiled and said, "You made a wise decision, Chollie." Crook recklessly stuffed the documents and the coin back into his bag and zipped it up, negligently catching the parchment paper in the zipper as he did so.

"Crook, stop! cried Mr. Pock. "You've crinkled my Declaration of Independence!"

Sam could maintain his silence no longer. He and his brother approached the two men and Sam said, "I wouldn't worry too much about the Declaration, Mr. Pock. It's a phony, just like the other items and the character who tried to dump them on you."

Why did Sam think this?

answer

Bob Crook spun around to behold the two detectives. Never at a loss for words, he began, "Well, well, well, Chollie. If it isn't 'Mr. Nobody' and his brother Noah. How long have you been standing there?"

"Long enough to hear you try to pass off those laughable 'artifacts' as authentic," said Sam with an air of self-righteousness.

"Laughable?" said Bob Crook. "You don't know what you're talking about!"

Mr. Pock silently watched the two men argue back and forth. He was eager to find out what made Sam think the items were not genuine.

"Well," said Sam. "Let's start with Mark Twain's birth certificate. He was born Samuel Langhorne Clemens. He used Mark Twain as a pen name. So what are the odds that an authentic birth certificate would have him as Mark Twain? It's even less likely that it would have him with the middle name, 'Steve.'"

"Well, I never said..."

"You certainly did, Crook," snapped Sam. "Also, I'd love to see you explain to me how the makers of your 'authentic' Roman coin happened to stamp the date 45 B.C. on it. B.C. stands for

Before Christ. This would mean that they had to know somehow that Christ would be born 45 years in the future."

"Well, it doesn't have to..."

"It certainly does, Crook," continued Sam, unfazed. "And finally, your most ridiculous item: an authentic, type-written Declaration of Independence. Do you honestly think that Thomas Jefferson clacked out the Declaration of Independence on a typewriter? Typewriters weren't even invented until almost 100 years later, you idiot! You might as well have said that Jefferson e-mailed you a copy."

Sam didn't realize how much fun he was having until he finished his diatribe, when he noticed that both Bob Crook and Mr. Pock stood listening to him speechless. Finally, the reporter picked up his satchel and started to shuffle dejectedly out of the office. Once, he turned to ask Sam a question, but as he opened his mouth, Sam put up his hand and sternly intoned, "Adios!" as if simply to brush him aside.

This seemed to give Bob Crook a jolt. He grabbed his head and pulled a blue headache pill out of his pocket, which he promptly swallowed. Then, turning defiant, he looked at Sam and fired off, "Fine, have it your way, Chollie. But you may want to check the headlines in Sunday's paper. I think you'll find them very interesting!"

"Why is that?" asked Sam.

"Adios!" mimicked Bob Crook triumphantly, in the attitude of a four-year-old, as he skipped out of the office. From increasingly farther away, Sam, Noah, and Mr. Pock could hear the reporter singing "Adios! Adios!" in a childish, made-up tune.

The Intruder

When the sound of Bob Crook's singsong chanting had completely subsided, Noah and Sam resumed the conversation with a very bored and yawning Mr. Pock. "Mr. Pock, it's very important that we speak with Ms. Renz," said Sam. "Can you please tell her that we're here?"

"No, I can't," slowly uttered Mr. Pock. "She isn't in at the moment, and she told me to turn away all visitors. She's very busy today."

Sam said, "It's an urgent matter. When will she be back?"

"I'm afraid I really can't say. She could be gone for hours," replied Mr. Pock. Just then a crash was heard coming from inside Ms. Renz's private office.

"Not in, huh? Could be gone for hours?" said Noah sarcastically. "That's fine. Then we'll just wait for her in her office." By the time Mr. Pock could find the words to offer a protest, they had whisked past him defiantly. He pressed the intercom button and mumbled something.

As the junior detectives approached Ms. Renz's inner office, they heard noises coming from inside. Sam tapped on the glass, but there was no answer. He opened the door, but no one was in sight. The office was bright and cheerful and the smell of honeysuckle filled the room. The aroma was created by a small candle that had recently been extinguished. The walls were lined with light blue wallpaper with a small circular design; it made one feel slightly off-balance. There was a small and very orderly desk with a cozy leather chair at the back of the room with several comfortable guest chairs situated within easy conversational distance.

In front of the window was a floor-length aqua drapery that was completely closed. Sam nudged Noah on the elbow to get his attention. He pointed at the bottom of the curtain where two shoes were peering out. The two young men tiptoed toward the window and each placed a hand on the curtain. With a quick pull,

Noah and Sam opened the drapery to reveal the owner of the shoes. As the curtain parted, Sam and Noah gasped. Although her hands were covering her face, they instantly recognized the girl they had helped in the parking lot the day before.

"Felicia!" Sam blurted out. "What are you doing here?"

"I...I have to go," Felicia stammered. She tried to step around Noah, but he blocked her exit.

"Not so fast, Felicia," said Noah. "First you pump us for information about Mayor Ever, and now we find you hiding out in the election official's office. You have some explaining to do."

"I'm sorry. I didn't mean any harm," said Felicia. "I was just... I thought you were cute, so I was just flirting with you."

"Oh, really?" Noah retorted. "If I'm so cute, then why did you give me a fake phone number?"

Felicia turned white and almost began to look ill. "I'm not feeling well. Please, I must get out of here."

Sam joined in the conversation. "You're in serious trouble, Felicia. You better tell us why you're hiding out in the election official's office, or we're going to report you to Ms. Renz."

"Fine, report me, then," snapped Felicia. "I doubt my mother will mind that I was in her office."

Noah and Sam looked at each other. "Your mother?" said Sam. "Come on, you don't expect us to believe that, do you?"

"Let's see your driver's license, or some other form of ID," demanded Noah.

"I don't have my pocketbook with me. But I think I know a way I can prove to you that I'm Felicia Renz."

"Okay, I'll bite," said Noah skeptically, folding his arms across his chest. "Convince us."

"I can prove it if you can remember back to what the mailman said to me when we were talking yesterday."

How was this going to prove she was Felicia Renz?

"How could I forget?" said Noah. "I was standing three feet from you when the mailman asked you, 'Are you friends?' I thought it was odd he asked, and odder still that you said yes. Then he handed you a package. Why did he ask you if we were friends?"

"That's not exactly what he asked," replied Felicia. "I was hoping you'd misunderstood. He didn't say, 'Are you friends?' He said, 'Are you F. Renz?' He thought he recognized me because I just started working here. He had a package for which I needed to sign."

Sam said, "Well, even if you are the daughter of the election official, it still doesn't explain why you lied and tried to pump us for information."

"I think I can explain it," exclaimed Avery, as he barged into Carrie Renz's office, startling Noah, Sam, and Felicia.

"What are you doing here?" Sam asked.

"I came to tell you not to bother Ms. Renz. I talked to Mayor Ever and he told me everything we need to know."

"I'm glad to hear that," said Sam. "But can you explain why Felicia was pumping us for information. Do you know her?"

"No, I haven't had the pleasure of meeting her," said Avery. "But I can tell you that I've seen her before. She's the woman in the picture that Bob Crook retrieved from Quentin's trash, where she was smiling and holding Quentin's hand. He tried to pass her off as his niece, but I'm willing to bet she's Quentin's girlfriend."

"Ex-girlfriend," interjected Felicia. "He was just using me to help his campaign, so I ended it."

"So," Noah said, closing in on her like a prosecutor cross-examining a witness. "Spying on Mayor Ever for your boyfriend, Quentin! Very sneaky, but I will say, I like your style!"

"It's despicable," said Sam, grabbing Noah's arm and leading him from the room. Avery followed and, in the parking lot, he told his sons about Mayor Ever's second letter and that the mayor admitted to having an affair with the election official.

Avery lit a cigar, saying, "Noah, call Annie and ask her to do a search on the Internet for Felicia Renz. I don't trust that girl."

Noah called the office, but got only the answering machine. He then called her apartment and got Annie's voice mail. She didn't even answer her cell phone, which was very odd indeed.

"We'll have to try her again later," said Avery.

mystery *12

The Vanishing

Annie came to with the most excruciating headache of her life. The stabbing pain worsened as her body jostled to and fro. Annie opened her eyes to see only darkness: she was blindfolded. From the constant jarring and bumping, she knew she was lying in the back of a speeding car. She tried to move her hands to remove the blindfold, but they were tied tightly behind her back. She heard an off-key rendition of "Tie a Yellow Ribbon" coming from the front seat; it drowned out the Ray Conniff Singers on the radio covering the catchy 1973 hit by Tony Orlando & Dawn. Although he was before her time, Annie briefly wondered whatever happened to that good-looking Tony Orlando.

Annie didn't know whether to scream or be silent and pretend to be asleep. She tried hard to recall what had happened as images flooded her brain. She remembered retrieving some papers from the filing cabinet with her back to the front door...hearing the door open...turning around to see who was there...a piece of cloth pressed to her face by a strong hand...then total blackness.

Attempting to remain calm, Annie maneuvered herself to see if she could sit up. She discovered that if she tilted her head back far enough, she could see out from under the blindfold. She carefully and stealthily moved her body up slightly into position.

Annie saw the back of the driver's head and then looked out the window. To her left was a giant field and the sun setting on the horizon. To her right she saw a park with children running and playing. The speed of the vehicle made clear it was on a highway.

"GET YOUR HEAD DOWN! NOW!" commanded the driver. Annie was startled and ducked down immediately.

"Who are you? Where are we going?" asked Annie.

"Just keep down and shut up and you won't get hurt!" barked the driver. "I'm taking you down south for a few days. You'll be very comfortable as long as you don't try anything stupid. After the election is over, I'll let you go."

A brave young woman not easily frightened, Annie nevertheless worried about her family. Avery, Noah, and Sam didn't know where she was. What would they think? She had to do something. "I'm so thirsty," she said.

"Hang in there." replied the driver. "It'll be dark soon and I'll stop to get you some water." Annie didn't trust the driver's word about stopping soon. She thought, he's already lied to me once, so I can't believe anything he says

What did Annie think the driver was lying about?

answer

Annie decided to stay as comfortable as possible while she concocted an escape plan. She tried to figure out where they were going. Well, she thought, he said that we were driving south, but I know that can't be true. Since the setting sun is to my left, we must be heading north.

Annie then figured that since it was almost dark, it must be about 6:00 EST. She had been filing the papers in the office at almost 4:00 in the afternoon. She deduced that they had been driving for approximately two hours. Annie knew that there were many fields and parks that lined the highway in Jespo County, at the north end of the state.

Friday

The Campaign Manager

Zee Dotes, public relations entrepreneur and amateur magician, was busy developing a public relations strategy for his newest client. Zee was a skinny, wide-eyed spin-doctor with a fast tongue and an even faster pen. He sat in front of the computer in his cramped office with papers piled high all around the room. Some piles were only a few inches tall; others topped three feet or more. The six filing cabinets throughout the dank, gray little office were stuffed beyond capacity, their metal frames bulging with the force of the papers packed into them. A steaming half-eaten container of chicken chow mein sat on his desk. The thick bags under Zee's eyes were a result of his perpetual overwork.

Despite a very successful public relations business and the considerable work it would save him, Zee Dotes refused to hire an assistant. Most days, he ran around like a lunatic, answering phones, meeting clients, writing press releases, and much, much more. At times, Zee was so overwhelmed that he broke down and cried right in his office, rocking back and forth like a baby. It was very sad. And a little funny. But mostly sad.

Deadlines, impatient clients, a backlog of paperwork—all these things weighed heavily on Zee's mind. And this was before he'd decided to take on his newest client two days earlier. He was far too overworked to do it, but he couldn't help himself. How could he turn down a request from the mayor of Wellington to manage his campaign? It was too great an opportunity.

Zee had 26 other clients, all of whom he decided he could put off until the election was over. All but one, that is. Even though Zee was working on the mayor's campaign, he had one other equally important client—Quentin Milestone. Of course, Zee realized it wasn't ethical to manage the campaigns of both candidates, but he just couldn't say no. Besides, no one had to find out because both candidates wanted to keep Zee a secret.

Since having been hired the week before by Quentin Milestone, Zee had created a vicious campaign slandering the mayor both professionally and personally. When he wrote the television commercials attacking the mayor, he had laughed to himself about the poor loser who would have to respond to them. And now he was that poor loser. He had only four days to revamp the mayor's campaign.

How he now regretted having said those nasty things about the mayor. And the worst part was that, not only did he have to answer those attacks, he had to launch new ones against Quentin, and then defend Quentin against them. Zee took two aspirin.

Mayor Ever knocked on Zee's door, right on time for their 2:00 strategy meeting. The mayor cleared away some papers off a chair and sat down to discuss business. The two gentlemen had barely begun to talk when the telephone rang. "Competitive Edge, Zee Dotes speaking," said Zee.

It was Quentin Milestone, sounding very upset. "Zee, we need to speak right away."

"What's wrong?" asked Zee Dotes.

"I heard on the street that 'Mayor Never' hired himself some hotshot public relations expert. We need to talk! I'm on my way."

"Listen, Quen..." said Zee, almost forgetting that the mayor was sitting in front of him. "Quen't you come later instead? I have a client with me," he said, saving himself.

"No, I'll be right there," said Quentin, and hung up before Zee Dotes had time to protest.

Zee paled and started to tremble as beads of sweat formed on his brow. The mayor asked, "Is everything okay? You look awful. Who was that on the phone?"

"No, no, it's nothing. I'm fine. It was just Kelly's Deli bringing lunch. They got lost."

The mayor moved closer and said, "Zee, you look scared out of your wits. Would you like some water?"

Zee waved the mayor away. "No, I'm fine, I tell you. I think we better reschedule our meeting."

Mayor Ever smiled and said, "Don't forget, Zee. I'm the mayor of this town. I can help you. But you have to open up to me and tell the truth. Who was that on the phone?"

Why did the mayor think Zee was lying?

answer

"I'm not lying. Why would I lie to you?" said Zee.

"Well, I'm no detective," said Mayor Ever, "but it seems highly unlikely that you'd order lunch from Kelly's Deli when you still have a half-eaten carton of Chinese food on your desk."

The Confrontation

Zee scrambled to find a way out of this mess. If the two candidates were to see each other at his office, they would realize they had both hired Zee Dotes as campaign manager, and Zee would lose both clients, as well as his reputation.

He tried to come up with an excuse to persuade the mayor to leave, but nothing was working. It dawned on him then that he would have to do something drastic to get the mayor out. With no time to waste, Zee decided to try the first thing that came to his mind. He threw his hand up to his face and screeched, "Oww. Oww, my eye!"

"Your eye? What's the matter with it?" asked Mayor Ever.

"I...I don't know, it itches, it's tearing, I'm blind...I need help. Go get a doctor. Go now!"

"You're blind? Oh my word! I'll call 9-1-1."

"No! What are you, nuts? They'll send an ambulance!" cried Zee. But it was too late. The mayor was already telling the 9-1-1 operator of Zee's sudden blindness and giving the address. The ambulance was on its way.

"They're sending an eye specialist," said Hugh.

"You have to leave now. I don't like anyone seeing me like this." Zee was getting shaky.

"Nonsense. I'll wait with you until the ambulance..."

"Get out! Get out! I'm blind! My eye itches! Don't you hear me?" yelled Zee.

"Okay, okay, I'll wait outside. Calm down."

Zee didn't want Hugh hanging around at all, but at least he was going to leave the office. He said, "If you insist on waiting, then wait in the back of the building. Go now!"

Five seconds after Zee heard the door slam, he saw Quentin pulling up in his Oldsmobile. Zee quickly stuffed the mayor's papers under one of his piles. Quentin marched into Zee's office.

"Zee, we have to get to work. Mayor Never hired some hotshot to come after us. We need to be prepared."

Zee was visibly shaking. "Listen, Quentin, please, we have to do this another time. I need you to leave now."

"I can't go now, Zee. I'm very worried about that sneaky mayor." Quentin was practically screaming.

In the mirror facing the rear window, Zee could see Mayor Ever pacing back and forth outside. He jumped to his feet as panic threatened to overwhelm him. "No, you have to go! Now! I can't listen now! I can't."

"You can't listen? Why not?" Quentin was getting upset.

"I...can't...I can't listen," Zee needed to think quickly. Once again he said the first thing that came to his mind. "I can't listen, I can't hear." He clapped his hand to his ear. "Oww! My ear!"

"What? What's wrong with you?" asked Quentin, alarmed.

"My ear, my ear! It hurts. I have an itch. It's waxy. I'm deaf. You must go now, please! Get a doctor."

"You're deaf? This is terrible! How did this happen? Don't you worry, Zee, I'll get you help right away." Quentin picked up the phone and called 9-1-1. Zee could only sit there in horror as he listened to Quentin tell the 9-1-1 operator about the sudden deafness occurring at the same address as the sudden blindness just moments before. Another ambulance was dispatched.

"They're sending an ear specialist," said Quentin.

As Quentin hung up the phone, Zee looked in the mirror to see Mayor Ever heading resolutely toward the front entrance. He started hyperventilating. This can't be happening, he thought. The mayor entered the building and was about to step into the office when Zee shouted, "Quick! Under the desk!" He was desperate.

"Under the desk? Whatever for?" asked Quentin. Zee was trying to stuff Quentin under the desk as the door swung open and in stepped Mayor Ever. The two rivals were face to face, so to speak, for the first time in several years. They stared intensely, each daring the other to flinch first. Zee Dotes jumped under the desk, where he found a receipt he had been looking for since 1997.

"So, come to spy on me, have you?" accused Quentin.

"Me?" said the mayor. "How dare you accuse me of spying? How did you know I'd be here? Why are you following me?" The men's voices raised and the argument escalated quickly.

The frustrations of the past eight years had built to a boiling point. The rivals had accumulated such animosity toward each other that it took very little to set it off. This was the spark that ignited their anger. Before reason could set in, the two men began to struggle. Quentin soon gained the upper hand, as he got the mayor in a headlock. Quentin's back was to the window as the mayor's face was pressed against the glass.

The mayor struggled to speak. "This won't look good for you Quentin. I brought a television reporter with me, and he's outside the window right now, taping us."

"Nice try, Mayor Never," laughed Quentin, as he increased pressure on the headlock. "But I know you're bluffing."

How did Quentin know the mayor was bluffing?

answer

"What are you talking about? He's right outside with his video camera!" insisted the mayor.

Quentin chuckled. "I can see outside the window from the mirror on the opposite wall. There's no one out there." Quentin tightened his grip. "How's that feel, Mayor Never? I still have some moves from my old wrestling days."

Quentin was finally forced to break the hold when the mayor kicked him in the shin. "And I still have some moves from my old football days," the mayor retorted.

Quentin hobbled in pain as the candidates went at each other again. Quentin reached out to grab the mayor when his thumb accidentally poked into the mayor's eye, causing him to back into a wall. The mayor clutched his hand over his eye, howling in pain. "I can't see!" he screeched. Quentin lunged for him, but tripped and knocked the side of his head against an overstuffed filing cabinet. Quentin grabbed his ear and started wailing uncontrollably. Zee Dotes watched from under the desk.

At last, Mayor Ever and Quentin Milestone staggered in pain out of the office into the street, holding their eye and ear, respectively. The ambulances pulled up and the candidates were directed to the appropriate specialists.

Zee breathed a sigh of relief. "That was a close one," he said, as he settled into his chair, put his feet up on his desk, and finished eating his chicken chow mein.

Saturday

mystery *15

The White Lie

Annie awoke and tried to open her eyes. It took a few moments for her to adjust to the sheer whiteness all around her. She looked around to familiarize herself with her surroundings. She was in a small, rectangular room with bright white paint on the walls and stark white furniture. The glare in the room was maddening, as every stick of furniture and decoration was completely white. The white of the walls flowed so perfectly into the white of the carpet, it was difficult to discern where one ended and the other began. There were no windows. A bright white light in the ceiling provided the only illumination.

Toward one end of the room were two beds, perfectly made, with white bedspreads and white pillows. Annie lay on her side on one of the beds. For a moment, Annie thought she saw a streak of blue on the white pillow case, but upon closer examination, she discovered it was just an illusion. Off to the side, Annie could see a bathroom producing the same white glare as the rest of the room. A petite woman sat quietly in a corner of the room with her eyes closed. Her dark hair stood out in sharp contrast to the white room and her white shirt and pants. There was a closet on the other side of the room where a similar white shirt and pants were draped over a hanger. Annie assumed that these were for her.

Annie looked at the woman and asked, "Where am I?"

"Oh," said the woman, startled at Annie's voice. "You're finally awake. You slept soundly for quite some time."

"How long was I out?" Annie asked.

"I can't say for sure," said the woman. "There are no clocks and no windows. I don't even know if it's day or night."

Annie was confused. "Would you say that I was out for days or just a few hours?"

"Well," the woman said, "I would say that it's been about a day and a half. You've been so groggy that I'm sure you won't remember my feeding you. But this is the first time you've spoken."

"He must have drugged me," said Annie, almost to herself. "Where are we? What is this place? Who kidnapped me? Who are you?"

The woman looked sorrowfully at Annie. "My name is Nicole. Unfortunately, I don't have any other information. I have no idea where we are. I know what you're feeling. I was just like you when I first got here."

"When was that?" asked Annie.

Nicole thought for a moment. "I'm not sure, but I've been trying to keep track by food. So far, I have been served 59 meals. They slide food under the door on a tray. Assuming they give me three meals a day, I'd say that I'm here almost three weeks."

Annie shot to her feet. "Wait a minute. Three weeks ago the governor's daughter was reported missing. You're not Nicole Stewart, are you?"

"I am!" she blurted.

"This is incredible! I'm Annie Body. My father and brothers were hired to find you! Some idiot reporter gave out secret information in the newspaper, and they lost the trail of the kidnapper. Have you seen the man who took you?"

"No, I've never seen him. But he talks to me through the door sometimes." Nicole leaned over to Annie and whispered, "I have to tell you that he gives me the creeps. I get the sense that he is somehow watching me from out there."

Annie surveyed the room and noticed several places where a small video camera could easily be hidden. "That's very possible. Tell me, did he say why he kidnapped you?"

"No, he didn't. But he did tell me that he was releasing me after the election. When he told me that, I realized that this has something to do with the fact that my father is a big supporter of Quentin Milestone and has been campaigning for him for months. We received threatening letters, but just ignored them. I think the kidnapper is someone who doesn't want to see Quentin elected mayor."

Annie said, "Well, that doesn't make sense. He also told me I'd be freed when the election was over, but my family is very close with Mayor Ever. In fact, my father has been campaigning vigorously for the mayor."

"Another thing," said Nicole. "For some reason, the kidnapper thinks my name is Charlie. I tried to explain to him that that's not my name, but he doesn't seem to get it."

Annie lost all color in her face. "You mean 'Chollie?' He calls you 'Chollie?' "

"Yes, that's right, Chollie. Do you know who he is?"

"I think so." Annie's initial shock turned to anger.

Just then, the sounds of some commotion came from outside the room. The two women heard shoes treading on a wooden floor, whispering, and then a key jiggling in the lock. The door opened into the room and a young woman was pushed inside. She tripped and fell to the ground as the door was closed and locked behind her.

Annie and Nicole ran over to help the woman up. When they did, Annie saw that she was face-to-face with the mayor's gum-chewing secretary, Lori-Beth Sugarman. She was blindfolded and her hands were tied securely behind her back.

"Lori-Beth! They got you, too?" marveled Annie as she helped her to her feet and removed her bonds and blindfold.

"Oh, thank you for taking off that blindfold. I haven't been able to see anything for hours. Where am I?" asked Lori-Beth, chewing a slightly oversized wad of gum.

"I'm still trying to figure that out," replied Annie. "All I know is that we are somewhere north of Wellington. And I have a good idea who is behind all of this."

Nicole asked Lori-Beth, "Are you okay? You weren't hurt, were you?"

"No, I wasn't hurt, Nicole. At least I don't think so," said Lori-Beth. She appeared to be perfectly fine.

Lori-Beth produced a pack of Juicy Fruit gum from her pocket and gave a piece to each of her fellow captives. She took three pieces for herself and stuffed them into her mouth all at once. The new pieces were soon consolidated into the existing wad, creating a bulge in her cheek that shortly began to resemble a small goiter. Annie introduced Nicole to Lori-Beth and the three women sat around in a semicircle to trade stories.

"Tell me, Anna," said Lori-Beth. "Your family is in close with the Mayor. What do you know about his campaign plans? Any big surprises that he's planning at the last minute?"

"Is that all you can think about?" cried Annie, with alarm. "We're trapped here in this windowless room with no hope for escape and all you can talk about is the election?"

"Well, excuse me, Anna, for trying to take our minds off the situation," said Lori-Beth indignantly.

"Never mind about that," said Annie. "Tell us how you were kidnapped."

"Oh," said Lori-Beth. "There's not much to tell really. I was walking out of my apartment when some man grabbed me from behind and forced me into the backseat of a car. About an hour later, the car pulled up in front of this duplex and I was taken inside and thrown in here. I was scared for my life the whole time."

"That's awful," said Nicole to Lori-Beth. "We were all abducted in exactly the same way."

"Well, almost the exact same way, Nicole," Annie said. "The major difference between our stories and Lori-Beth's is that ours are true."

Why did Annie suspect that Lori-Beth was lying?

answer

"What are you talking about, Anna?" spluttered Lori-Beth. "You think I'm lying?"

"Of course you're lying, Lori-Beth," said Annie. "And I can't imagine why, but you're obviously in on Nicole's kidnapping, too."

"How do you figure, Anna?" asked Lori Beth.

"Well, for starters," Annie began, "you knew Nicole's name before I introduced you."

"So? She looks like a Nicole," retorted Lori-Beth, chewing wildly.

Annie nodded her head sarcastically. "I see. Then perhaps you can tell us how you knew that this place was a duplex if you were blindfolded?"

"That's simple," said Lori-Beth as she got up and walked the length of the room. "I was able to see the house even though I was blindfolded."

"And how was that possible?" inquired Annie.

Just then, Lori-Beth darted for the door and pounded insistently on it. A few seconds later, a key could be heard entering the lock. Annie had a good idea that Lori-Beth was about to escape, so she leapt to her feet and darted after her. Once the door was unlocked, Lori-Beth wasted no time jerking it open and slithering through.

Annie tried to grab onto the door as it was being pulled shut, but it was a losing battle. She tugged with all her strength, but felt her grip loosening. Determined not to let the door close, Annie slid her foot into its path. She emitted a piercing wail as the door closed on her ankle. At the same time, her foot was being kicked back into the room from the outside. She knew she didn't stand a chance and that the door would be shut and locked at any second. Thinking quickly, she grabbed the piece of gum in her mouth and wedged it into the lock on the side of the door. Her foot was finally kicked back into the room and the door slammed shut with a thud.

mystery *16
The Fancy Ladies & the Snoots

On the other side of the railroad tracks in Wellington, there resided a large segment of snooty, well-to-do people. In the past two elections, this influential group had supported Mayor Ever. These races had been so close, however, that without the all-important backing of these snoots, the mayor could not have won. Seeing the possibilities in this, Quentin Milestone was doing everything in his power to win over this affluent demographic in Wellington.

And it seemed that Quentin was getting help in this endeavor. Thursday morning, Wellington was descended upon by two impressively snooty older ladies from England—Mrs. Doila Valvington and Mrs. Suzy-Jean Silverspoon. The snooty Wellington crowd didn't know much about these newcomers except that they were very British, very snooty, and very, very fancy. Even though the fancy ladies had been in Wellington for less than a day, the town snoots looked up to them and respected their opinions. It had to be the accent.

Doila and Suzy-Jean were lunching at Chez Maison, the fanciest restaurant in town, where they were surrounded by an admiring group of snoots. Doila Valvington was wearing a large, frilly hat with pretty flowers in it. She looked very fancy indeed as she sipped her cappuccino, one finely manicured pinkie raised elegantly skyward. Suzy-Jean Silverspoon also wore an appropriately large, colorful, and frilly hat. In addition to flowers, however, hers contained a diamond pin and several pieces of fruit. In the corner of the restaurant, not far from their booth, a heavily bandaged Quentin Milestone was seated at a table, hidden behind a tall plant.

"You know," Doila Valvington addressed the onlookers in a ritzy British accent, "we've just arrived in your town today from England and rented an apartment. And though we may not know much about your politics, I think it's pretty clear who is the better candidate."

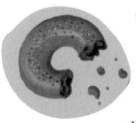

The onlookers were clinging to her every word, among them, Kathy Dwyer, chief snoot of Wellington. She said, "Pardon me, ladies," and although she had never been to England, Kathy suddenly spoke with a British accent. "I certainly don't mean to doubt your word, but you just arrived in town today. How could you know so quickly that Mayor Ever is the better candidate?"

The fancy ladies were aghast. "Did you say Mayor Ever?" asked Suzy-Jean, in evident surprise. "Surely you jest. I believe Mrs. Valvington was referring to that dashing hairstylist, Quentin Milestone."

A stunned silence filled the air, followed gradually by whispers of increasing volume, and climaxing in a loud frenzy of chittering, yapping, and general snootery. Suzy-Jean continued, "In fact, I wouldn't vote for that rude, obnoxious Mayor Ever if he were the only candidate on the ballot!" Behind the plant, Quentin smiled broadly.

Kathy Dwyer wanted to defend Mayor Ever, but she couldn't bring herself to disagree with so elevated an authority as the British ladies. She ventured timidly, "But what makes you think that Mayor Ever is rude?"

Doila Valvington took a dainty little sip of her cappuccino and placed her cup back on the dainty little saucer. "We ran into the Mayor just a short time ago. Mrs. Silverspoon and I walked out of our apartment and waited in line for the elevator. When it stopped at our floor, we got on and saw Mayor Ever on his way down."

Suzy-Jean continued the story. "We recognized him from the posters hung up all over town. We introduced ourselves and then the mayor insulted us. He said, 'We don't need you pompous British ladies in our town. We have enough pompous people here as it is.' "

This scandalous piece of gossip had a tremendous impact on the Wellington snoots; it immediately soured their opinion of the mayor. They found it appalling that he would refer to them as pompous. It appeared as if that one statement might alter the outcome of the election.

The two fancy ladies continued to make harsh comments about the mayor as they enjoyed their fancy coffee beverages. Between sips and snipes, the opinionated socialites dabbed the corners of their mouths with their napkins. As Doila Valvington was making a particularly astute comment regarding the Mayor's taste in clothing, she was interrupted by a pungent odor and a tremendous fist crashing abruptly on the table. Both the fist and the odor belonged to the owner of Greg & Eric Plumbing Contractors, John Reed. John was wearing a dirty white tee shirt and a tool belt around his ample waist.

"Good afternoon, ladies," said John. "I couldn't help but overhear your conversation and your comments about the mayor. Mind if I join you?" John began, casually wiping his runny nose with the back of his hand.

The fancy ladies were taken aback by John Reed's lack of social graces. Before they could answer, John was maneuvering his rather large buttocks into the seat next to Suzy-Jean.

"Scooch down a bit, would ya?" John had powdered sugar around his mouth and was holding a donut.

"Ooh, is that a caffachino?" asked John. "Mind if I dunk?" Not hearing a refusal, John dipped his half-eaten jelly donut into Suzy-Jean's cup of cappuccino, kept it there a minute (to "soak up the juice"), swirled it around, and then removed it, tapping it gently against the cup to drain back the excess liquid. John Reed audibly expressed his enjoyment as he took a man-sized bite out of the donut.

Doila Valvington began to fan herself to stop from fainting. Suzy-Jean Silverspoon did a double-take so fast that a tangerine became dislodged from her hat and catapulted clear across the room, almost knocking Quentin Milestone unconscious.

John said, "I just got done fixing the bathroom sink when I came out and heard you two broads talking. Now, I don't know nothin' about you dames, but it's plenty clear that you're a couple of fakes." He took another healthy bite out of the donut.

The fancy ladies shifted in their seats and began to look a bit uncomfortable. The Wellington snoots held their breath and watched the ladies closely, waiting for them to deny the accusation, and possibly even give John Reed a splendidly indignant tongue-lashing. But the denial didn't come.

Finally, Kathy Dwyer became suspicious; she asked the ladies what they had to say in response. Doila Valvington and Suzy-Jean

Silverspoon were utterly humiliated. They said nothing at all, just shot a most unfancy look of hatred at John Reed.

Why did John Reed think the ladies were fakes?

His mouth full of donut and his chin sporting a goodly bit of jelly, John Reed explained what he meant. "You see, I ain't never been to England or even London, for that matter, but I do watch a lot of Monty Python. And the one thing I know about them Englanders is that they talk funny. I heard you two say that you rented an apartment and saw the mayor on the elevator. Well, in England, they don't call it an 'apartment;' they call it a 'flat.' And no Englander would ever say 'elevator;' to them, it's a 'lift.' Also, Brits don't wait in a 'line;' they wait in a 'queue.'"

John took one last dunk into Suzy-Jean's beverage and stuffed the remainder of the donut into his mouth. He stood up and clapped his hands repeatedly to shake the powdered sugar from his fingers.

"It's been a pleasure, ladies. Now I have some pipes that need fixin'." John tipped his plumber's cap and disappeared.

The mortified faces of Doila Valvington and Suzy-Jean Silverspoon had deepened several shades. In no time at all, they were up from the table and out of the restaurant. As Suzy-Jean trotted down the street, she left behind a pitiful trail of grapes and figs from her fancy hat. Quentin Milestone, seeing the fancy ladies—whom he had hired—hurtle out of the restaurant, sat in the corner with his face in his hands, more grateful than ever for the shelter of the tall plant.

The Campaign Ads

The nature and the pace of the campaign were getting increasingly brutal in its final days. The residents of Wellington were inundated by a cascade of news updates, commercials, and billboards. Wherever one looked, there was another ad for one of the candidates or a poll indicating the voters' changing sentiments. It was getting out of hand.

If the mayor placed an ad on a taxi, Quentin had to put one on the side of a bus. When Quentin put up a billboard, the mayor countered by hiring a skywriter to paint "Mayor Ever Forever" in the clouds. Soon the entire town was plastered with Mayor Ever and Quentin Milestone propaganda. Bumper stickers, flyers, sandwich boards, lawn signs, posters, they were everywhere! Some of Quentin's hardcore supporters even carved the letter "Q" out of the hair on the backs of their heads. It was simply maddening.

But the worst of all—the most horrifying aspect of the entire campaign—was the television commercials. What began as tame barbs against their opponents' political views soon escalated into full-fledged character assassinations. Each candidate was buying expensive commercials and unleashing brutal, slanderous attacks against the other.

Although Avery had been campaigning intensely for his friend Hugh, he decided that he had to try to put a stop to the attacks. He surreptitiously arranged to bring Quentin Milestone and Hugh Ever together to end their childish displays of one-upsmanship once and for all. The meeting was to be held at Avery's office that evening at 8:00 sharp. Avery tried to get Annie to set up the meeting, but she was nowhere to be found. He had to make the arrangements himself.

Since it was just one day after the brawl in Zee Dotes' office, both candidates were still recovering. The Mayor was the first to arrive. His left arm was in a sling and a black patch covered his right eye.

"You look awful!" noted Avery. "I had no idea it was so bad. I heard it was nothing serious."

"Nothing serious?" echoed Hugh. "Are you kidding me? The man practically blinded me, and you say it's nothing serious?! From the time he gouged my eye yesterday until only about two hours ago, I couldn't see a thing out of either eye. Total blackness. I call that serious. Just wait until the press hears about this. I'll make sure they see Quentin Milestone for the animal that he is!"

"Well, Hugh," said Avery in a soothing voice, trying to calm the Mayor down, "that's why I invited you here this evening...." Before Avery could continue, the door to the agency opened and in came Quentin Milestone.

"Wait just a minute," snarled Hugh. "What's *he* doing here?"

Quentin was no less unpleasantly surprised. "Excuse me, Avery. But you didn't mention that you were inviting Mayor Never along. What is this anyway?"

If possible, Quentin looked even worse than the mayor. He had a specially designed bandage on his ear that covered a good part of his head, and the movement of his neck was restricted by a brace. To compensate for a severe limp, Quentin walked with the aid of a crutch under his left arm.

The two men moved closer to one another and were soon standing face to face. They practically growled, each daring the other to break the stare first. Avery kept the rivals from each other by inserting his massive self between them.

"The reason that I called you gentlemen here today was to put an end to this childish bickering," Avery said. "Your incessant, slanderous attacks are tearing this town apart, and I will not allow it any longer."

He maneuvered the two men into his private office and shut the door. "Now, you two are going to stay here until we come up with a solution. All night, if necessary." Avery locked the door and put the key into his pocket.

"Avery, you don't understand," pleaded Hugh. "The man sent me to the hospital. I hate hospitals! The food was lousy and the nurses were so mean. The redheaded nurse I had this morning was even worse than the blonde nurse I had last night. And Quentin Milestone is responsible for it!"

"I was just defending myself," asserted Quentin. "Hugh kicked me so hard in my right shin, I thought it was broken. The man used to play football! Then he shoved me head first into the filing cabinet. I almost went deaf!"

Avery put up his hand. "Enough! Don't you see what you're doing? I insist that the two of you end this immediately or I will see to it that the newspapers find out that the mayor has been dating the election official and the challenger has been dating her daughter. Do I have to tell you what that would do to the two of you in the polls?"

Both candidates were outraged. "You wouldn't do that to a friend, would you?" said Hugh.

"You wouldn't dare!" sneered Quentin.

"I certainly would," replied Avery, "if the two of you don't stop faking your injuries and put an end to these slanderous attacks."

Why did Avery think they were faking?

answer

"What are you talking about?" exclaimed Hugh.

"Faking? You think we're faking these injuries?" asked Quentin.

"Of course, you're faking," accused Avery. "Hugh, you told me just five minutes ago that you couldn't see a thing until this morning."

"That's true!" said Hugh.

"Then how did you know that your nurse last night was a blonde?" Hugh was silent.

"And you, Quentin," continued Avery. "You claim that Hugh kicked you in your right shin, yet you walk with a crutch under your left arm."

After a long pause, the mayor removed his eye patch and Quentin took off the bandage from around his ear and the brace from his neck.

"Well?" asked Avery. "Are you two going to drop this nonsense and start acting like mature adults?"

Quentin reluctantly offered his hand to Hugh. Hugh just as reluctantly shook it.

"I have an idea," said Avery. "This calls for a celebration. Let's have a drink and some cigars." The two abashed candidates agreed.

Avery walked over to a cabinet and produced an expensive bottle of whisky that he had been saving for a special occasion. One drink turned into two, then another, then another. As the bottle emptied, relations between Hugh and Quentin became much more relaxed and friendly. When they were completely inebriated, the two opened up to each other, admitting everything.

By the end of the long evening, the candidates were confessing to their secret affairs, to having spied on each other, and to countless other rule infractions and crimes that they had never expected to divulge. The three of them finally passed out at around 6:00 in the morning.

Sunday

The Leak

The three men slept soundly in Avery's office early that Sunday morning. Hugh and Quentin were sprawled out in Avery's comfortable leather chairs, while Avery himself was slumped over his desk, snoring up a storm. The sound of the telephone ringing shattered the morning's peaceful silence. Avery, with his head next to the telephone, shot to his feet with a start. Quentin and Hugh stirred in their chairs but did not awaken. Avery looked at the clock. It was 7:00 A.M. Oh my, only one hour's sleep, Avery thought. He cleared his throat and picked up the phone. In a groggy and almost incoherent slur, he said, "Busih-budda-tective-agency."

Sam was talking frantically on the other end. "Did you see today's newspaper?" He was practically in tears. "How could this happen? What are we going to do?"

Still in a stupor, Avery mumbled, "What? I'll check the paper and call you back."

He hung up the phone and staggered to the door past Hugh and Quentin, sleeping undisturbed in their comfy chairs. Avery took the key out of his pocket and opened the door to his office. What a hangover, he said to himself. Avery opened the front door of the agency and picked up his copy of *The Daily Sentinel* on the stoop. He peeled off the rubber band and uncurled the newspaper. He looked at the front page to see the following headline glaring at him: "Candidates Admit to Secret Affairs, Crimes, and Unethical Behavior."

Avery couldn't believe what he was reading. He shook his head and rubbed his eyes to focus better. Then he read it again, hoping it would be different. But it wasn't.

His heart sank as he read the article:

During an all-night drinking binge at the Busy Body Detective Agency, Mayor Hugh Ever and his opponent, Quentin Milestone, admitted to past crimes and improper affairs during this year's mayoral race.

The mayor confessed to having a secret affair with Carrie Renz, Wellington's election official, a revelation that has left the town stunned. There is suspicion that this romance could have influence on the way the election is conducted.

To complicate matters, his opponent, Quentin Milestone, admitted to having a secret affair with the election official's daughter, Felicia Renz, a woman half his age. Foul play is also suspected by the Milestone camp.

Although neither of them has officially dropped out of the race, the polls will reflect a tremendous decline in support for the two candidates. If this continues, Wellington will be left without any viable candidates for mayor. An unnamed source, however, has indicated that there may be a new last-minute contender.

Avery could bring himself to read no more. He brought the paper into his office and tried to rouse Hugh and Quentin.

"Get up! Get up!" He started shaking the men, who were just beginning to show signs of life. Avery ran to the water cooler and filled two large cups with ice water. He ran back and splashed it in the faces of Hugh and Quentin. The two men screeched in shock and jumped up from their chairs.

Avery began to shout, "Get up! Get up both of you! This is an emergency! Look!" He held the newspaper up for them to read. "Look at the headlines!" The two candidates gaped in disbelief.

"I'm ruined!" shouted Hugh. "You've ruined me, Milestone! I never should have trusted you!"

"Me? It was you!" cried Quentin. "I can't even go out in public now. They'll destroy me! Why did you do this?"

"Avery, you have to believe me. I had nothing to do with this!" pleaded Hugh. "It must have been Quentin! He sneaked out when we were asleep and called the paper!"

"I did nothing of the sort, you lunatic!" protested Quentin. "Avery, he's the one who called the newspaper. I had nothing to do with it!"

"Relax, both of you," said Avery. "I don't know how the newspaper got wind of the story, but I can assure you that neither one of you had anything to do with it."

Why was Avery so sure?

answer

"What do you mean, Avery?" asked Hugh. "Do you mean to say that it was you?"

"No, no, of course not," assured Avery. "We were all here together last night until we finally passed out around 6:00 this morning. The newspaper had already been printed long before that. Besides, neither of you could have left the room. The door was locked and the key was in my pocket all night long."

This seemed to quiet down the candidates. Avery continued, "And, don't forget, the information in the article damages both of you. I doubt either of you would have disclosed your own secrets."

The three men paced around the office trying to figure out how this could have happened. The candidates realized that this could be the end of their campaigns. They had to put some damage control into motion, and quickly. They left Avery's office in a panic.

Fly, Avery, Fly

Avery couldn't figure out what do to. He decided to call his family in for an emergency meeting. He had no problem getting in touch with Noah and Sam, but Annie still could not be found. When his sons arrived, they sat down in his private office and started to have a brainstorming session.

Avery began, "There have been some strange occurrences in the past week that I can't explain. First, there's the mayor's letter." He pulled the letter out of the drawer and examined it. "The mayor said that he wrote this letter himself to persuade us to investigate Quentin Milestone. But then the second letter arrived, and it was similar in wording to the first letter." Avery pulled out the second letter from the same drawer and compared the two. "Hugh denies having written this letter, and I believe him. The handwriting is completely different in the two letters."

"You mean...?" said Noah.

Avery and Sam waited for Noah to finish his sentence, but they knew he had nothing else to say. Sam continued, "But we were the only people who knew about the first letter. Who else could possibly have written it?"

"That's what we have to figure out," answered Avery.

"Maybe he told his secretary, Lori-Beth Sugarman," said Sam.

"Maybe," said Avery. "But Hugh told me that he was too scared to tell anyone. I think that you're onto something about Lori-Beth, however. I know she's hiding something."

Noah chimed in with his redundant guess. "Maybe he told his secretary, Lori-Beth Sugarman."

Avery and Sam looked at Noah in amazement, ignoring the comment. Avery went on, "And now there's the story in today's newspaper. Hugh, Quentin, and I were the only people who could possibly have known what was being discussed in the office. I know I didn't leak the story, and, obviously, neither of them could have leaked it."

Noah and Sam offered suggestions that ranged from the mildly illogical to the outright ridiculous, including talk of alien abductions (Noah's idea). As they mulled over their theories, Avery was deep in thought, recalling the visitors who had been in his office over the past week.

And then it hit him. His heart skipped a beat as he remembered an incident that had taken place several days earlier. He walked over to where Sam was sitting, reached his hand under the chair, and felt around. A moment later, Avery gasped. He stood up and frantically waved his arms at his sons.

Seeing their father act like a lunatic made Sam and Noah begin to worry. "What's going on?" asked Sam. "Are you okay?"

Avery put his finger to his lips to quiet his sons, and began to talk in a strange and animated manner. "Oh, well, you know...you see, I, um, I've decided to talk to Hugh about dropping out of the race immediately." As he said this, he shook his head from side to side and flailed his arms in the air, trying to indicate that he didn't mean it.

"What are you talking about? You can't do that!" exclaimed Sam.

"Are you okay?" asked Noah. "Why are you waving your arms around like that?"

"Who me?" said Avery. He attempted a forced laugh. "Ha-ha, no, my arms are perfectly still. As I was saying, I think I'll talk to Hugh right away about quitting politics for good. It's the best thing now that all this dirt is out." Avery looked like an enormous madman gesturing wildly with his arms and shaking his head violently from side to side. It almost looked as if he were attempting to fly. His frantic hand signals seemed to make no sense, so his sons just sat there, getting more and more worried about their father.

Why was Avery acting this way?

Noah finally stood up and grabbed Avery's arms. He couldn't stand the sight of his father losing control. Then Avery had an idea. He shook loose from Noah and reached into his desk to pull out a piece of paper. He grabbed a pen, and in big letters wrote the word "bug."

Noah nodded his head in seeming understanding and immediately left the room. Sam got the clue and decided to play along. "Oh, yes, of course, that's the only right thing to do. Get Mayor Ever to drop out of the race. Yes."

As Sam said this, Avery motioned for him to continue. The two of them carried on this very fake-sounding conversation for several minutes. Just then, Noah burst into the office with a can of Raid and began spraying indiscriminately. Avery and Sam darted out of the office with Noah following close behind. When they were in the reception area, Avery explained what was going on.

"You see, boys, I thought back to all of the people who were in my office recently, and I remembered an incident that occurred when Bob Crook visited us on Tuesday. As he was leaving, I remembered that he dropped his notebook, and I saw him reach his hand under the chair to pick it up. I didn't think anything of it at the time, but it dawned on me just now that he might have been planting a bug."

"Oh, a *bug*!" said Noah, hiding the Raid behind his back.

Sam said, "So that explains the letters. Bob Crook must have heard you read the first letter and then wrote a second one to sound like the first. But why?"

"I don't know," replied Avery. "But it also explains how *The Daily Sentinel* was tipped off about last night's conversation among Hugh, Quentin, and me. Bob Crook heard the whole thing and then wrote the article for his newspaper."

"That sneak!" said Noah. "Pretty clever, if you ask me."

"No one asked you," said Avery. "And, for some reason, Hugh's secretary is in on it as well. When she handed Hugh the second letter, she said it contained bad news. But the envelope was sealed. Obviously, she knew the contents of the letter before it was ever opened."

"We should have a word with his secretary then," suggested Sam.

Avery nodded in agreement. "Excellent idea. Let's ask Annie to get her address, and we'll pay Ms. Sugarman a visit. Where is Annie, by the way? I've been trying to get in touch with her."

"I haven't seen her for a couple of days," said Sam. "I tried her on her cell phone, but there's no answer."

Avery was getting worried. "This is quite disturbing. She always answers her cell phone. I've never seen her without it. Where could she be? She isn't home; I called there this morning. Try her cell phone number again."

Noah picked up the phone and dialed Annie's cell phone. The three detectives were startled by a faint ringing from the closet. They followed the sound, opened the closet door, and saw Annie's pocketbook on the floor. Sam opened it and pulled out her ringing cell phone. Avery's face paled. "Noah, call the police," he said.

mystery *20

The Cheesy Policemen

"Did you call the police, Noah?" asked Avery some time later.

"I sure did. They said they'll be here any minute," replied Noah.

Avery nodded in approval. "Did you ask for Chief Wilkins?"

"Yes," said Noah, "and he's sending two of his best men."

"That's good," said Avery. "As you know, Chief Wilkins and I go back a long way. I'm sure he won't let us down."

Avery paced around the reception area wringing his hands. The wrinkles in his forehead were more pronounced than usual.

The three of them began to discuss the last time they remembered seeing Annie. "It was three days ago," Avery said. "Hugh was here with his secretary when he came to show me the second letter. We all left the office, and Annie was by herself."

From the window in the reception area, the three detectives saw an unmarked car pull up and two official-looking gentlemen get out and walk into the building. From the office door, Avery motioned for the gentlemen to enter. They did so and the taller of the two men said, "Good morning, my name is Detective Stanley, and this is Detective Echo, my assistant."

Detective Echo said, "I'm his assistant."

The two detectives shook hands with the three Bodys and had the following dialogue:

Avery: Thank you for coming so quickly.

Detective Stanley: Just doing my job, sir.

Detective Echo: Just doing his job, sir.

Detective Stanley: So do I understand rightly that somebody is missing?

Avery: No, that's not accurate.

Detective Stanley: Somebody isn't missing?

Avery: Of course not, Sam Body is standing right over there. You just met him.

Sam waved.

Detective Stanley: Hold it. We just received a call about a missing person here. Is this a hoax? You're telling me that nobody is missing?

Detective Echo: Nobody is missing?

Avery: No, I didn't say Noah Body was missing. He is standing right next to Sam.

Noah waved.

Detective Stanley: I'm confused. Let's start again. Did anybody call the police?

Avery: No, of course not, Detective. Annie Body is missing, probably kidnapped. I doubt the kidnapper would have let her call 9-1-1.

Detective Stanley: Well we're here, aren't we? Somebody must have called the police!

Detective Echo: Yeah, somebody must have called the police.

Noah: Why is that, Detective? Do you think I'm too stupid to pick up the phone and call the police?

Avery: I assure you, Detective, that both of my sons are fully capable of operating a telephone and calling the police.

Noah: And I'm pretty good at calling long distance, too.

Sam: You should see him fax.

Detective Stanley: Enough already! I'm here to investigate a missing person, not to play Abbott and Costello.

Detective Echo: Third base.

Avery explained Annie's disappearance to the detectives and the circumstances surrounding the election. Avery said, "You know, I am the owner of a private detective agency, so I have some expertise in this field. I have a feeling that her disappearance has something to do with the election."

Detective Stanley looked around the office and said to Avery, "Do you have any cheese?"

"Cheese?" repeated Avery.

"Yes, cheese," said Detective Stanley. "Detective Echo loves cheese."

"I love cheese," confirmed his assistant.

"No," said Avery. "I apologize. I don't believe we have any cheese."

"Gouda, cheddar, American, Swiss, he's not picky," said Detective Stanley.

"I'm not picky," echoed Detective Echo.

"Like I said, I do not have any cheese in the office," Avery repeated. "I'm sorry."

"Any kind of cheese will be fine," persisted Detective Stanley. "Munster, brie, camembert, Roquefort, goat, string, blue, toe...."

Avery was getting suspicious. "Tell me, Detective Stanley, why did Chief Wallace assign you to this case? Do you have expertise in missing persons?"

"Yes, that's exactly right," said Detective Stanley. "Chief Wallace knows our track record of finding missing persons, so he sent us. But we really do need cheese to do our jobs effectively."

"We need cheese," said Detective Echo.

"Well gentlemen, I thank you both for coming out to see me, but I think we'll wait for the real police to arrive."

What on earth was Avery talking about?

"The real police?" asked Detective Stanley. "What makes you think we're not real? Is it the cheese?"

"Not at all," said Avery. "I happen to know for a fact that some police officers do indeed enjoy a nice hunk of cheese now and again."

"It's hard to resist. You do admit that," insisted Detective Stanley.

"Yes, I do admit that," agreed Avery.

"Write that down, Echo, he admits it."

Detective Echo pulled out his pad and said it as he wrote, "Cheese...is...good."

"So how did you know?" asked fake Detective Stanley.

Avery said, "I asked you if Chief Wallace assigned you to this case. You said that he did."

"What's wrong with that?" Stanley wanted to know. "Why wouldn't Chief Wallace assign us to the case?"

"Because there is no Chief Wallace," Avery answered. "His name is Chief Wilkins."

As Avery finished his explanation, the sound of a police siren could be heard approaching. Within seconds a squad car pulled up in front of the building and two officers started to emerge. They were getting out of the car when fake Detectives Stanley and Echo turned to see them coming. Fake Detective Stanley said, "Uh-oh, Echo, it's the fuzz. Cheese it!" They made a move for the door, but the officers beat them to it.

One of the officers opened the agency door and walked in. "Well, look who's here," said the officer. "If it isn't Mr. Stanley and Mr. Echo. Let me guess. Listening to the police radio again?"

"I don't know what you mean," insisted Stanley.

"Tell me, did you get any cheese out of them this time?" the officer said.

"No, no cheese," said Stanley.

The officer walked closer and said, "Now, I thought I told you that I didn't want you two playing detectives any more. If I see you pulling this again, I'm going to have to bring you in. Understand?"

The fake detectives nodded and meekly left the agency. The officer addressed Avery. "I hope they didn't cause you any stress."

"I'm overwhelmed with the stress of a missing daughter," said Avery, proceeding to tell the officers every detail of the case.

"Don't worry, Mr. Body. We'll put out an APB and search every nook and cranny in this town," assured the officer. Avery Body looked sorrowful as he thanked the officers and watched them leave. Then he turned to his sons.

"We can't rely on other people to find Annie. We have to put our heads together and come up with a plan."

The three of them paced around the room, Avery with his head down and his hand on his chin. Seeing how impressive this classic strategizing pose was, his sons assumed the same position.

"If only there were some kind of clue," wished Avery. As he said that, he spied a piece of paper lying behind Annie's desk. He reached around the desk as far as he could and grasped it with his pinkie and thumb. He gently eased the paper forward until he had a grip on it and pulled it out.

"This must have fallen behind Annie's desk." It was a note similar to the one Hugh Ever had brought to him three days earlier. Avery read it aloud:

Avery Body, you scum! How dare you help that no-good Hugh Ever in the election! Don't you know that he's a putrid pool of puke? Stay out of it! Keep your trap shut! I'm here in your agency right now to deliver a warning to you and your idiot sons. Stay out of it!

To make sure that you keep your gigantic nose out of this election, I've taken the liberty of kidnapping your daughter. If you ever want to see her again, MIND YOUR OWN BUSINESS! Hold on, your phone is ringing. I'm back. It was your accountant, call him tomorrow, you're late filing your quarterly return. I'm warning you! Stay out of it!

Sincerely,

Anonymous

P.S. I love what you've done with the office!

Avery's face turned crimson with rage. He pounded his fist into his hand over and over, saying, "If I get my hands on that lowlife reporter, I'll strangle him!" Avery tore the letter to shreds, ignoring the fact that it would be needed for evidence.

"What makes you think it's Bob Crook?" asked Noah.

"Because, Noah," Avery explained, "the last letter Hugh received was exactly like this one. And we've already established that Bob Crook wrote it, mimicking the first one that Mayor Ever wrote. We've got to find him before he hurts Annie."

Sam jumped up and marched toward the door. "What are we waiting for? Let's get the creep!"

"Hold it," said Avery. "We need a plan. Sam, you drive to the newspaper to see if he's there. Noah, you check his apartment. And I'll see if I can locate Lori-Beth Sugarman. Make sure you keep your cell phones on, and call me if you find anything."

The detectives left the agency focused on finding their Annie.

The Triple-Cross

Hugh Ever was practically in shock when he left Avery's office that Sunday morning. All his careful planning and diligent campaigning were for nothing because a nosy reporter had taken it upon himself to publish the details of his personal life. Most upsetting of all was that this was happening just two days before the election. In fact, the very day before, the polls had shown the mayor leading with 52% of the vote. Now, he would be lucky if he got 52 votes in total. Both he and Quentin Milestone had lost their credibility and the respect of their fellow citizens—the voters—overnight.

But Hugh had never given up anything very easily. He made the decision that if he were going to lose the election, he would go down swinging. Despite a terrific hangover, he left the agency and got into his car. He turned on the engine and pulled out of the parking lot, intending to go see his campaign manager, Zee Dotes.

As he sped down the highway, he came upon a sight that left him breathless. On the northbound side of the road was a prominently placed billboard featuring the gigantic, smiling face of Bob Crook, the reporter who had broken the story in *The Daily Sentinel*. Underneath the picture of the smiling Mr. Crook was a caption reading "Crook for Mayor."

The sight of it made Hugh's blood begin to boil as he pressed his foot to the gas pedal. His blood pressure rose proportionate to his car's speed as he continued toward Zee Dotes' office. He noticed more and more billboards advertising Bob Crook for mayor. Until that morning, many of those same billboards had had Hugh's or Quentin's faces on them. All he could think about was getting even with that punk reporter.

As he pulled into the parking lot of Zee Dotes' public relations agency, he noticed Quentin Milestone's Oldsmobile parked in front. Hugh parked his car and stormed up to the front door, from where he could clearly hear a fierce argument taking place within. He was about to pound on the door when he noticed that it was open. Hugh entered the office unnoticed.

Quentin was holding a copy of *The Daily Sentinel* in Zee's face. "Didn't you see today's newspaper?"

Zee Dotes was backed against a wall, cowering. "No, no, I told you, I didn't see the paper! What's it say? Is it bad?"

"Of course it's bad, you idiot!" replied Quentin, bringing the rolled-up newspaper vigorously down on the side of Zee's head. "Why do you think I'm screaming at you? It trashes me and Hugh Ever. We're both ruined! And why is Bob Crook's face on my billboards? How can you let this happen to me? You're my campaign manager. You should have stopped it! As far as I know, we're both off the ballot. And I blame you!"

Quentin was in a rage and he looked dangerous. Zee trembled and braced himself for a further attack. He remembered how vicious Quentin could be from the fight he had witnessed between him and the mayor just a few days earlier. He had to think quickly to save himself.

"No, no, it's okay," pleaded Zee, as he held his hands out to protect himself.

"What's okay? What are you talking about?" shouted Quentin, with fists clenched.

"It's all okay. Everything is alright. I just got off the phone with the election official not five minutes ago, and he told me that you're still on the ballot!"

"Oh, he told you that, did he?" said Quentin sarcastically.

"Yes, just before you came in. So you see, there's nothing to worry about," said Zee, hoping to calm Quentin.

"You're wrong, there's plenty to worry about," said Quentin. "And there'll be even more to worry about if you don't stop deceiving me."

Why did Quentin think Zee Dotes was lying?

"I'm not deceiving you, Quentin!" insisted Zee. "Why would you say such a thing?"

"Because..." began Quentin, but before he could speak further, Hugh Ever stepped into Zee's office from the reception area.

"Because," said Hugh, picking up where Quentin had left off, "I have been dating the election official for the past three months, and I can say with absolute certainty that the election official is not a 'he.'"

"So it's obvious you didn't speak to the election official," said Quentin.

"What is also obvious," said Hugh, "is that you've been double-crossing both of us. Haven't you, Mr. Dotes?"

"No! Not at all," said Zee, forcing a casual laugh.

Mayor Ever was closing in on Zee. "When I hired you to be my campaign manager, you didn't tell me that you were already Quentin's campaign manager."

"Is this true, you little worm?" asked Quentin.

"Wait, I can explain," pleaded Zee. "Yes, I admit it. It's true. I worked as campaign manager for both of you. But I worked very hard to represent you both fairly and to the greatest advantage."

"What about all of those attacks in the newspaper?" asked Hugh. "Was it you who called me a 'fat-headed boil' in Thursday's editorial section?"

Zee looked Hugh in the eye and said, "Well, yeah, I wrote that. But I had to get back at you for calling Quentin a 'mindless moron' in Wednesday's paper."

"I never called him that. You did!" barked Hugh.

"Well, yes, I did," admitted Zee. "But I couldn't very well let him get away with referring to you as an 'overgrown pygmy' in Tuesday's paper, now could I?"

"I've heard all I can stand," said Quentin as he grabbed Zee by the collar.

In desperation, Zee lifted a big plastic sign from his desk and held it in front of his face for protection. At the sight of it, Quentin's heart skipped a beat and Hugh's face blanched. In thick black letters it read, "Bob Crook for Mayor."

"This is too much!" said Hugh. "You're Bob Crook's campaign manager, too?!"

"I have to earn a living!" screeched Zee. "Besides, he made me an offer I couldn't refuse."

"And what was that, exactly?" demanded Quentin, releasing his grip on Zee's collar.

"He offered me some priceless museum pieces if I promised to be his campaign manager," said Zee. He walked behind his desk and picked up a blue duffle bag. "See?"

He opened the sack and pulled out the items to which he was referring: an authentic Mark "Steve" Twain birth certificate, an authentic Roman coin dated 45 B.C., and an authentic type-written Declaration of Independence.

"He said I'd be the envy of Wellington!" Zee insisted.

To appease the outraged candidates, Zee gave away the birth certificate and the coin, but kept the Declaration for himself. The Mayor and Quentin went away satisfied.

The Gumshoe
& the Gum-Chew—Part I

On his way to Lori-Beth's apartment, Avery also glimpsed the billboards advertising Bob Crook for mayor. Now it's all starting to fall into place, he reasoned. All along, Bob Crook has been trying to ruin Hugh and Quentin so he could step in and run away with the election, Avery was thinking, as he pulled in front of Lori-Beth's apartment building amid a torrential downpour.

Avery wanted to wait for the rain to abate before leaving his car, but he didn't have any time to spare. He needed to find Annie's whereabouts. He stepped out of his Cadillac and prepared to make a run for it. As fast as his stocky legs could carry him, Avery darted for the apartment building. Although it took him only a few seconds to reach the building, he was soaked from head to toe. He chastised himself for forgetting to bring an umbrella.

Lori-Beth's apartment was on the ground floor, the first on the left as soon as you entered the building. Avery rang the doorbell. He waited a few seconds for a response, but there was none. He pressed his ear against the door, but couldn't hear a peep. He rang the doorbell a second time and followed it up with a rapid succession of knocks. After thirty seconds of silence, he was convinced that no one was home.

I'm going to have a look around, thought Avery. He reached into his wallet and produced a credit card. After sliding it into the crack between the door and the jamb, Avery wiggled the card until he felt the lock give way.

"It's good I know a thing or two about the gentle art of lock picking," he mused.

Once the lock was picked, Avery hastened to enter the apartment and shut the door. Although it was daytime, the rainstorm rendered the room fairly dark. He didn't want to turn on the lights in case Lori-Beth came home; she might see them in the window or under the door. Instead he pulled a small flashlight from his pocket and started to explore the apartment.

Avery walked into the living room and swept it with his light. Wherever he aimed his flashlight, it fell on balled-up gum wrappers. Discarded packages of Juicy Fruit, Bubble Yum, and Doublemint littered the carpeted floor. An old-fashioned gumball machine stood in the corner.

Avery went right to work. He opened drawers, cabinets, boxes —anything he could get his hands on—to look for clues. He found an address book in a desk drawer and took it out. Before he could open it, though, he heard footsteps coming down the hall outside.

Avery froze for a moment, seeking a hiding place that could accommodate his size. As the doorknob turned, Avery bounded over to a window in desperation, where he took the shade off a lamp and placed it on his bald head. He stood there shaking like a leaf as the door opened and Lori-Beth entered the apartment.

The instant she turned on the light, Lori-Beth emitted an eye-bulging, ear-piercing scream, seemingly induced by the sight of her drawers hanging open and her possessions strewn about. Avery trembled beyond control, his heart pounding in his chest. He was afraid that, like the man in Poe's *Tell-Tale Heart,* his throbbing heartbeat would reveal his hiding place. But it didn't.

Instead, as soon as Lori-Beth looked around, she caught sight of an enormous, dripping-wet man standing under a tiny lampshade that barely covered his hairless head. He trembled so convulsively that the shade was nearly dancing there.

Without warning, Lori-Beth delivered a tremendous blow that crushed into Avery's midsection. He doubled over and the shade went flying off his head, exposing him completely.

"Mr. Body!" gasped Lori-Beth. "What's going on? Why are you pretending to be a lamp? I didn't hurt you, did I?"

"No, no, not at all," said Avery, struggling to collect his breath. "Well, I better be going now..."

"What are you doing here? How did you get in?" Lori-Beth wanted to know, as she worked her mouth on an impressive wad of pink gum about the size of a golf ball.

"I..." Avery was at a loss. He wasn't about to admit that he had broken into her apartment. "I was passing by and I noticed a small fire inside your window. So I climbed in and put it out. That's when you walked in." Avery thought of a missing detail and smartly added, "Oh, and then I put the lampshade on my head." Avery seemed very satisfied with his story.

"Mr. Body, I may not be a trained investigator like you, but even I can tell that your story doesn't make sense."

How did Lori-Beth know?

"Now, why you would think that, Lori-Beth?" asked Avery. He was not accustomed to being in this position. Normally, Avery was the one who caught others telling lies; now he was getting a taste of his own medicine.

"Well," said Lori-Beth, pausing to indulge in a few thoughtful chews, "if you came in through the window and put out a fire just before I walked in, there wouldn't be these water tracks all over my carpeting leading from the door to the window."

The Gumshoe & the Gum-Chew—Part II

Avery blushed as he realized that he had been caught. "I'm sorry for not being honest, Lori-Beth. The truth is that I'm really quite desperate. You see, my daughter is missing."

"Anna is missing?" asked Lori-Beth. "I'm sorry to hear that."

"It's Annie," corrected Avery. "And I think that you may be able to help me find her."

Lori-Beth seemed eager to help. "If I can, I'll be happy to, Mr. Body. In what way can I help you find Anna?"

"Annie," said Mr. Body.

"What about Anna?"

"There is no Anna. Her name is Annie," insisted Avery.

"Oh, well, if you say so, Mr. Body. She's your daughter. But I think you're wrong." Lori-Beth walked over to the gum dispenser and turned the knob two full rotations. She reached her hand to the bottom of the machine and scooped out a handful of gumballs. She was about to add them to the existing wad, but changed her mind. She got rid of the old gum and started a new wad with the fresh gumballs.

"Lori-Beth, when you visited my office the other day with Mayor Ever, he told me that you had handed him a letter that morning. Do you remember that?"

"I remember," replied Lori-Beth.

As they spoke, Lori-Beth gathered articles of clothing, cans of food, and other miscellaneous items, and put them into a small case. It appeared as if she had just stopped back home to pick up a few odds and ends.

Avery continued, "The mayor said that when you handed him the letter, you mentioned that it contained bad news. But the envelope was sealed. How did you know what was in the letter?"

"You got me there, Mr. Body," said Lori-Beth. "I haven't a clue. How did I know?"

"I don't know how you knew," said Avery. "I'm asking you."

Lori-Beth looked confused. "Yeah, I don't know. It was sealed. How could I have known what was in it?"

"Exactly. How could you have?" asked Avery.

"That's what I've been saying," replied Lori-Beth.

Avery shook his head in disbelief. He decided to try a different approach. "Tell me. Lori-Beth, where could I find your friend, Bob Crook?"

"Friend? That's a good one," said Lori-Beth. "I hate the guy. He just said that he would hire me as his secretary when he's elected mayor."

"But you're already the Mayor's secretary," Avery pointed out.

"Yeah, but he said he would double my salary." Lori-Beth blew a huge bubble to emphasize her statement.

Avery was getting agitated. "Lori-Beth, what kind of help did Bob Crook ask of you?"

"I better not say any more, Mr. Body," said Lori-Beth. "I said too much already. I'm sure he won't hurt Anna, Mr. Body. She looked just fine to me." She grabbed her bag and made a move toward the door. "You can lock up when you go, or just leave through the window if you prefer."

"Wait! You saw Annie? When? This morning?"

"Like I said, Mr. Body, I have to go." Lori-Beth tried to walk around him.

"Is that where you're going now?" asked Avery excitedly. Lori-Beth didn't respond. "Did you see her this morning? Is that where you were?" Still she remained silent. "Tell me, Lori-Beth, is that where you just came from?"

"No, not at all. I just came from the dentist," said Lori-Beth. "I had a couple of cavities filled. Now, I really must be on my way."

Avery figured he would try a different strategy. "Okay, Lori-Beth," he said. "I'm sorry I ever doubted you. Have a lovely day."

He stepped aside to let her pass and Lori-Beth hurried out of her apartment. Avery waited a few seconds before he followed her. He casually climbed into his Cadillac and turned the ignition. Avery gave Lori-Beth a few seconds' head start and then took off after her.

"At the dentist," Avery said aloud. "That's a good one! With any luck, she'll lead me right to my Annie."

What's wrong with Lori-Beth's story?

answer

Avery could see that Lori-Beth was about a tenth of a mile ahead of him on the road. He kept her in sight while making sure not to follow too closely. Avery called his sons on his cell phone and told them to get in their cars. He said that he was hot on the trail of Bob Crook and would give them directions once he knew more.

Avery had a hunch. He told his sons to contact Governor Stewart to tell him to be on alert. Avery put down his cell phone and concentrated on following his target as he replayed the last conversation with Lori-Beth in his head.

The dentist, indeed! thought Avery. Even if her dentist were open on a Sunday to fill her cavities, I doubt that she'd be able to chew gum with a face full of novocaine.

The Great Escape

Annie waited until she and Nicole could hear nothing from outside the door. It had been at least ten hours since Lori-Beth darted from the room and Annie wedged a small wad of gum in the side of the door. When it was completely silent and Annie was convinced that no one was near, she grabbed the doorknob, hoping that the gum had jammed the lock.

The gum had indeed done the job: Annie was able to pull the door open without turning the knob. She peered through the crack. It was pitch black. Annie was unable to see even two feet beyond the door. She knew that they had to make a move immediately, as this might be their last chance to escape.

While Annie was plotting her escape, Lori-Beth Sugarman was busy leading Avery Body to the hideout. Avery was careful to stay several cars behind Lori-Beth so she would not notice him tailing her. He got on his cell phone again and called Sam.

"We're turning off of Yukon and heading north on Highway 9. I want you to call the police for backup, and make sure you keep the governor posted," he instructed.

After waiting what seemed like an eternity, Annie opened the door enough to slide her slim body through and then motioned Nicole to follow suit. When the two women had cleared the door, Annie closed it shut. The two captives tiptoed across the floor, searching with their hands for a wall or a door. Suddenly a light switch was flicked and the entire room lit up brilliantly. A scream escaped Nicole as Annie froze in her tracks.

When Annie's eyes adjusted to the brightness, she saw that she was in a large white room with broken-down furniture. This room was as stark as the previous one, with the same blinding glare. Nicole was at her side, gripping her arm. Sitting in a chair across the room was Bob Crook, wearing his famous derby and an irritating smirk. In front of Bob Crook, Annie could see a table on which lay a number of items. She noticed a cold compress and a magazine in the center of the table, some green pills and a glass of water to the right, some red pills to the left, and a large gun hanging off the edge of the table.

"Congratulations for getting out of the room, Chollies," said Bob Crook. "Now you've presented me with a problem. Since you've seen who I am, there's no way I can let you go when the election's over, as I promised. I'm going to keep you a while longer until I figure out a plan. I have a migraine, so I'm going to ask you both not to give me any trouble and I'll take it easy on you."

Nicole fell to her knees and began to plead with Bob Crook.

"It's no use, Nicole," said Annie. "He's a cold-hearted criminal. Your cries won't sway him."

Annie attempted to reason with him, but she got nowhere. She wracked her brains to think of a way out. She decided that if she saw Bob Crook pick up the gun, she would rush him and scream for Nicole to make a break for it. At least one of them might make it out alive.

Meanwhile, Lori-Beth pulled off the highway and was working her way through side streets until she came to a dirt road, where she turned in. Avery waited until she was far enough ahead and then pulled in after her. In the distance he could see a house. Avery got back on his cell phone to give Noah and Sam his exact whereabouts. They were close behind.

Avery stopped about 100 feet from the house. He waited for Lori-Beth to get out of her car and start walking toward the front door. Avery got out of his Cadillac and stealthily lumbered closer. His heart was pounding with the anticipation of soon confronting his daughter's kidnapper.

Inside, Annie hoped her unyielding stare would show Bob Crook that she couldn't be intimidated. She thought back to the first time she had met him. Suddenly, it dawned on her that she might be able to use against him something she had learned about him then. No wonder everything is white, she mused.

Annie took a deep breath and charged toward her kidnapper.

In an instant, Bob Crook sprang to his feet. Annie lunged for the table as he grabbed for the gun. She was too late, as Bob Crook snagged the gun and fumbled it. Annie knocked into the table, scattering its contents. Bob Crook pointed the gun at her head and commanded her to stand up and move back. As she stood, Annie used the table to steady herself and quickly rearranged the remaining items. He ordered her to stand against the wall.

Bob Crook sat down, grabbed his head, and started bobbing back in forth in pain. "My head! It's pounding!" he groaned.

He took a pill from the right side of the table and swallowed it, followed by the glass of water. Then he stood up and paced around the room, waiting for the pain to subside.

"What are we going to do?" whispered Nicole to Annie. "He's going to kill us!"

"He's not going to kill us," replied Annie, also in a whisper. "Just give it a minute and we'll be safe."

Why did Annie think that?

answer

Lori-Beth walked in the front door, Avery just a few feet behind her. As Lori-Beth entered the house, she heard Avery's footsteps. She shrieked and tried to slam the door shut. With a burst of energy, Avery caught the door with both his hands and overpowered the gum-chewing secretary. He looked around; seeing the light and hearing the voices coming from the next room, he darted for it.

Crook was stumbling around and tripping over his feet, but managing somehow to keep his balance. "I don't feel so good. What's happening to me?"

His knees buckled and he wobbled to and fro. "What color was that pill I took? Was it green?"

Annie smiled and said, "Actually, I think it was red."

"Oh, no," was his response.

Annie mocked a look of sympathy. "Sorry, Chollie."

Avery entered the room, saw Bob Crook, and rushed toward him. Avery clenched his fist and brought his arm back. With all the strength he could muster, he drove his fist in the direction of Crook's face. Just as Crook lost his balance and began his descent to the floor, Avery's fist met Crook's nose. Crook hit the ground with a thud.

"I've still got it!" cried Avery proudly, as he rushed over to Annie to see if she was okay.

Very shortly, cars could be heard pulling up to the house. In a flash, the house was filled with policemen. Noah and Sam came running in, followed by Governor Stewart. When Nicole saw her father, she started to cry and ran into his arms.

The next day, the story was everywhere—in the papers, on TV and radio—how Avery Body had single-handedly foiled a kidnapping ring, saving both his own daughter and that of the governor. Overnight, Avery became the biggest sensation that Wellington had seen since Morey Amsterdam filmed a television special there thirty years earlier.

When Annie read the account in the paper, she smiled to herself. She was quite content to let her father take all the credit for knocking out Bob Crook, when, in fact, it was she herself who had caused him to do so.

Annie had remembered that Bob Crook was color blind, and that he was unable to distinguish his green headache pills from his red sleeping pills. When she rushed him, she wasn't after his gun; her intention was simply to switch the pills on the table. Moments after he took the wrong pill, he was out cold.

On this point, the good citizens of Wellington easily reached consensus: Avery Body was a true hero. Mayor Ever, as one of the last acts of his term, declared that the day before election day would forever be known as "Avery Body Day." The town council held an emergency session and proclaimed that Main Street would be renamed Avery Body Boulevard.

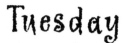

Tuesday

The Election

Wellington was a small town with a population of slightly less than 15,000. The number of registered voters totaled 8,532. Each election day, four voting booths were wheeled into the gymnasium of the Louise Graham Elementary School (named after the first schoolmarm in Wellington 148 years before). The process was usually very orderly with voters coming in and out of the school all day, from 7:00 A.M. to 8:00 P.M. This year, however, the operation ran a little less smoothly. Instead of the residents voting sporadically throughout the day, they all converged upon the school at once, early in the morning. It seemed as if the entire town were there.

Across the street in Sophie's Diner, the fancy ladies, Mrs. Doila Valvington and Mrs. Suzy-Jean Silverspoon, regarded the bustling activity. Not being residents of Wellington, they were unable to vote. So they just sipped their fancy coffees and looked out the window.

The two ladies surely outdid themselves with fanciness that day. The weight of Mrs. Valvington's hat strained her neck muscles in the very effort to keep it aloft. It was adorned with jewelry, flowers, pins, renderings of the English monarchy from 1066 to the present, an IOU from a dear, dear friend of hers, an unopened letter from her first husband (a major in the Salvation Army—a major!), a six-inch high platinum apostrophe, and, of course, fruit.

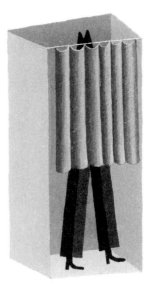

Not to be outdone, Mrs. Silverspoon's hat was equally ostentatious. In addition to the same items found on Mrs. Valvington's hat (the jewelry, flowers, pins, drawings of the English monarchy from 1066 to present, an IOU from a dear, dear friend of Mrs. Valvington, an unopened letter from Mrs. Valvington's first husband, a six-inch high platinum apostrophe, and fruit), she had assorted vegetables and a small statue of a financial analyst.

The two ladies had a clear view across the street. They saw Avery standing outside the elementary school, chatting with Governor Stewart. Zee Dotes was sucking up to the governor, probably hoping to win him as a client in the next election. Annie and Nicole stood together by the entrance as Noah and Sam flirted with Felicia Renz in the parking lot, attempting to outcharm each other in the hope of winning her attention.

A long line of townspeople waited to vote and Molly Peltin, the hairdresser from the Top Cat, was near the front. After much contemplation, she had decided to vote for her boss, even though she was being paid by the mayor to spy on him. In the middle of the line stood fake Detectives Stanley and Echo, the latter snacking on a sticky, melting block of gorgonzola. Behind them, the town snoots were led by their queen snoot, Kathy Dwyer.

Inside the school, Carrie Renz and Mr. Pock supervised the proceedings. The commotion was intensifying, the excitement building. It was nearing fever pitch when a limousine pulled up in front of the school. The crowd grew quiet as they waited to see the passengers. The driver got out to open the passenger door. A moment later, Mayor Ever emerged wearing a yellow tuxedo and top hat. Coming out directly behind him was his rival, Quentin Milestone, dressed in a matching yellow tuxedo and top hat. The crowd gasped as the two men walked together toward the school.

As the two distinguished gentlemen slowly made their way, the waiting crowd parted to clear a path for them. The mayor opened the door for his opponent and stood aside for him to pass. Quentin graciously tipped his hat and proceeded to walk through. The mayor followed.

Avery was very pleased to see this. He joined ranks with them in moving toward the booths to show support for his old friend Hugh, and to demonstrate his approval of the new cordiality between the candidates. The townspeople were happy to let the candidates cut in line and Avery's new status as a hero won him the same privilege.

As the mayor and the challenger walked toward the voting booths, the residents silently beheld them. How nice it was to see two old rivals walking side by side in friendship on this climactic day. Both the mayor and Quentin smiled and waved to those they knew, amiably shaking hands and exchanging words of greeting. Only the snoots gave Mayor Ever the cold shoulder as he walked past, not having quite forgiven him for his alleged insult.

Fake Detective Stanley patted Quentin on the shoulder and fake Detective Echo offered him a piece of cheese. Not wanting to be rude, Quentin accepted. The crowd took delight in seeing Quentin hold out his hand for a piece of Echo's sticky gorgonzola. Not to be outdone, Mayor Ever also extended his hand, but fake Detective Echo was reluctant to part with any more. He finally relented and let him have a piece. The candidates ate the melted cheese and looked around for napkins. None could be found.

As they approached the front of the room, Mayor Ever tipped his hat to his girlfriend, Carrie Renz, the election official. She smiled at him but scowled at Quentin, having discovered that he had been secretly dating her daughter. Hugh and Quentin walked toward the voting booths and turned to face the growing crowd. The constituents began to whisper until Quentin lifted his arms to quiet them. Moments later, the room was silent again.

The Mayor took a step forward and cleared his throat. Surveying the crowd's rapt faces, he said, "Citizens of Wellington, we would like to thank you all for coming today to exercise your rights as Americans. The race for mayor has been unfortunate, characterized by scandal, animosity, and negativity. That is why we have come here today together. My opponent, Quentin Milestone, and I have decided that, no matter who wins, the other will pledge his support. Our goal is to make this town the best it can be."

The announcement was followed by a murmur, then sporadic clapping. Within seconds, it grew to resounding applause throughout the gymnasium, finally reaching a crescendo. This is when Quentin stepped forward and raised his arms again. When it was quiet once more, he addressed the crowd.

"As my esteemed opponent said, we are here together to demonstrate solidarity of purpose in the mutual support of our beloved Wellington, and to show that we have put aside our petty differences. To emphasize my point, I will now enter the voting booth to cast a vote for my new friend, my opponent, Hugh Ever."

The mayor then stood next to Quentin and said, "And I will enter the next voting booth and likewise pull the lever for my new friend, Quentin Milestone."

Again the crowd broke into applause. Not since almost thirty years before, when Morey Amsterdam was run out of Wellington for breaking the town's ordinance on spitting, had this town rallied for a cause. People hooted and whistled as the applause continued.

Both Hugh Ever and Quentin Milestone stepped into the voting booths and pulled the curtains. A few seconds later, the light in the mayor's booth went off, and he opened the curtain and walked out. Almost immediately, Quentin's light went off, and he too emerged from his booth. As the crowd cheered and clapped, Avery entered the closest booth, the one just used by the mayor to cast his vote. When he came out, he walked over to the one just used by Quentin and peeked inside.

By this point, the clapping was beginning to die down. The mayor then addressed the crowd. "As the mayor of this fine town for the past eight years, I have had the pleasure and honor of serving you. It has been the happiest eight years of my life. Thank you, Wellington!"

Once again applause filled the gymnasium. Glowing with the exhilaration of the moment, Mayor Ever turned to Avery and said, "See, Avery? Everything works out in the end. And you know, I had no reservations whatsoever about voting for my opponent."

"Oh, no?" remarked Avery. "Perhaps that's because you didn't vote for your opponent. You voted for yourself."

"He what?!" shouted Quentin incredulously. "Back to your old tricks again. I should have known never to trust you!"

"I wouldn't talk if I were you, Quentin," said Avery. "You also voted for yourself."

Why did Avery think that?

answer

"How dare you accuse me of such a thing!" protested Quentin. Hugh echoed the complaint.

"Don't forget, gentlemen," said Avery, "that I voted immediately after you, and I used the same booth that you did, Hugh. I also sneaked a peek into the voting booth that you used, Quentin."

"So?" said Hugh. "The votes are wiped clean once the curtain is opened. You couldn't have seen who we voted for."

"Well, the votes may have been wiped clean," answered Avery, "but the levers weren't. I saw sticky cheese on the lever for Hugh Ever in your booth, Hugh, and I found the same sticky cheese on the lever for Quentin Milestone in the booth that Quentin used."

Epilogue

One week later

Avery was in his office, sitting back in his chair with his feet propped up on his desk. He was on the telephone with his old friend, Mack Gray, with whom he had been friends since college. Avery was telling his friend about the election.

"After I caught them in a lie about their voting for each other, the two of them began a shouting match. They went from best of friends to sworn enemies again in less than fifteen seconds."

"It was that bad, was it?" said Mack.

"Let me put it this way," said Avery. "When they found out they had each voted for themselves, they tried to run back into the same booth to vote again. They struggled like animals until the booth tipped over and fell on the floor."

"Who finally won?" asked Mack.

"It was a real mess," said Avery. "As it turned out, the election ended in an almost perfect tie. Quentin Milestone was ahead by a mere 180 votes. Well, there was no way that Hugh was going to let that stand without a fight, so he demanded a recount. When he recovered 209 votes, Quentin demanded a recount of the recount. There were serious questions concerning election tampering involving Hugh and the election official, and Quentin and the election official's daughter. Both candidates were going on about hanging chads, pregnant chads, and dimpled chads. There was even confusion about some voters who claimed they had accidentally voted for Morey Amsterdam. Finally, Governor Stewart had to step in and come up with a solution."

"What did he do?" asked Mack.

"He picked someone from the town to serve as interim mayor, until we can hold a new election next month."

"Who'd he pick?" asked Mack.

"For some reason," Avery said "he picked this public relations guy. No one can figure out why. His name is Zee Dotes."

Mack laughed. "Zee Dotes? You're kidding me, right?"

"No, why?" asked Avery. "Do you know him?"

"No, it's not that," said Mack, still chuckling. "I'd just love to be around to hear someone call him 'Mayor Zee Dotes.'"

Avery had to think about it only a moment before he got the joke. He shared a hearty laugh with his old friend as he opened up his silver humidor and selected a nice, thick stogie.

☛ • • • • • • Meanwhile, upstate at the Governor's Mansion, Governor Keith Stewart was alone in his study. He had locked the door for privacy before he reached under his desk to pull out a blue duffle bag. He opened the bag and carefully pulled out its contents. He sat back in his chair to examine his new possession.

"I can't believe it," he mused aloud. "An authentic typewritten Declaration of Independence! I'll be the envy of everyone at the next Governors' Convention!"

☛ • • • • • • And so ends the saga of the race for mayor of Wellington. Mayor Zee Dotes managed to hang on to his position by his usual means of fast talking and tricky advertising. Quentin Milestone returned to his barbershop and Hugh Ever took a job making sandwiches at Kelly's Deli. Both men patiently bided their time, shaving faces and buttering bread, respectively, counting the days until the next election, just a short four years away.

Index